HOW TO MAKE YOUR

LIFE

MORE

EFFECTIVE

HOW TO MAKE YOUR

LIFE

MORE

EFFECTIVE

HERBERT
LOCKYER

WHITAKER
HOUSE

All Scripture quotations are taken from the King James Version of the Holy Bible.

Boldface type in the Scripture quotations indicates the author's emphasis.

How to Make Your Life More Effective
(Previously published as *How I Can Make My Life More Effective*)

ISBN: 978-1-62911-185-8
eBook ISBN: 978-1-62911-186-5
Printed in the United States of America
© 1955, 2014 by Ardis A. Lockyer

Whitaker House
1030 Hunt Valley Circle
New Kensington, PA 15068
www.whitakerhouse.com

Library of Congress Cataloging-in-Publication Data (Pending)

1 2 3 4 5 6 7 8 9 10 11 12 **W** 22 21 20 19 18 17 16 15 14

CONTENTS

PREFACE

When commissioned to prepare this book, it was made clear that the production of a volume for the individual who has a forty-hour work-week in which to make his living, but who desires to put some of his spare time into the work of the Lord, was desired.

These individuals have the matter of their livelihood taken care of, but want to dedicate their hours away from the daily tasks to forms of service enriching the lives of others. How amazing are the activities of the multitudes of unpaid, spare-time laborers in the Master's vine-yard! One has only to think of church office bearers and members of lay groups, of the Gideons, of the Christian Business Men's movement, and of similar organizations, to realize how much the cause of Christ owes to a vast host of unselfish, unpaid workers. May their tribe increase upon the earth!

> Master, I have not strength to serve Thee much,
> The 'half-day's work' is all that I can do,
> But let Thy mighty multiplying touch

Even to me the miracle renew.
Let five words feed five thousand, and Thy power
Expand to life-results one feeble hour."
—Frances Ridley Havergal

The writer hopes he has succeeded in his assigned task, and that the following chapters will serve to prove how effective one's life can be when only a part of it can be devoted to sacred ends. Secular occupations have to be undertaken by the overwhelming majority of Christians. They must have regular employment in order to provide for themselves and others. The time away from their vocation, however, is their own, to dedicate or dissipate. They are wise who know how to give "each flying minute something to keep in store." All of our time, even part time, as we call it, must be redeemed, seeing the days are evil.

1

THE MYSTERY OF LIFE

Before we consider the question, "What is your life?" it is imperative to know what we mean by the mysterious possession we call *life*. The term is used in many ways, as *Webster's Dictionary*:

1. The vital force, whether regarded as physical or spiritual, the presence of which distinguishes organic from inorganic matter.

2. Conscious existence, conceived as a quality of the soul or as the soul's nature and being.

3. The state of that which is alive, or the fact of a living being.

4. The duration of a life.

5. An individual human existence…as, each day of one's life.

6. A way or manner of living.

7. That which imparts or excites spirit or vigor—life of a company—night life.

In our own employment of the term, we have in mind the vital force and conscious existence called "life" revealing itself in the noblest deeds through the way or *manner* of life. The *matter* and the *manner* of life are inseparably bound together in man. There cannot be a way of life without *life* itself.

Between "life" and "existence" a shade of difference can be discerned. The latter applies to all created things. The former is the property of only some created things to whom it has been communicated. Whatever has life has existence, but there are many things that have existence but no life. The biblical conception of life implies that it is active, never inert—something that every living person possesses, needful for his or her purpose, the source of which is God, the Living One. It is He who originates and sustains our mortal lives. Life emanates from Him: *"In him was life; and the life was the light of men"* (John 1:4).

All scientific attempts to explain life, or to produce life apart from God, have failed. Man has not been able to create even the simplest form of life or to see it rise spontaneously. If it be true that "all life comes from life," then our first parents must have received their life from God, as we believe they did. He is the Living God, the original Source of all life. As the Eternal One, He did not receive life from some prior source.

Unbelieving scientists, however, deny this evident fact of Scripture. The source of life, they say, is some blind, mechanical force operating in nature. Godless science claims that life originated as a result of the synthesis of inorganic elements into organic compounds through the action of natural laws. Is it not easier to believe that it is in God we live, move, and have our being? (See Acts 17:28.)

Scientists, we are told, have recently "prepared a crystalline protein, which possesses the properties of tobacco mosaic virus. The protein has a larger molecule than egg albumen, is insoluble in water, and its properties remain unchanged after ten successive crystallizations. But on the living tissue supplied by a tobacco leaf, the protein apparently becomes a virus that can reproduce itself independently....If there is even a possibility of the synthesis of new life today, how much easier the whole process must have been in lost limbo of earth's history in the late Azoic or the early Archaeozoic eras." Such a boast of science is tantamount to saying that life can be produced out of lifeless substances. But the Bible declares that God alone is the Source and the Giver of life. He is the One endowing man with life: *"And the* LORD *God formed man of the dust of the ground, and breathed into his nostrils the breath of life; and man became a living soul"* (Genesis 2:7). Other things had life before Adam appeared. There was organic life in the grass and the trees of the fields, which God had created. Life gave these inanimate objects their shape and capacity for growth and reproduction. In the beasts, fishes, and fowls, there was not only *organic* life, but also *sentient* life, in that they were able to move: *"And God said, Let the waters bring forth abundantly the moving creature that hath life, and fowl that may fly above the earth in the open firmament of heaven"* (Genesis 1:20). They were able to realize pleasure and pain, and, in some cases, contribute to the beauty and harmony of the surrounding universe.

The life with which God endowed Adam, however, was of a higher reach in the scale of life. The ox and the ass have knowledge, including memory and a capacity for reflection sufficient to enable them to distinguish one thing from another: *"The ox knoweth his owner, and the ass his master's crib: but Israel doth not know, my people doth not consider"* (Isaiah 1:3). But man has a faculty for reasoning with God, which beasts have not. As Henry Thorne points out, "The cattle browsing on the hillside may 'nourish a blind life,' but man, even when debased and sinful, has what is known as 'perceptive faculty.' Once the mind, shrouded by the mists of guilt, is clarified by the Spirit, the invisible things of God can be clearly seen: *'For the invisible things of him from the creation of the world are clearly seen, being understood by the things that are made, even his eternal power and Godhead; so that they are without excuse'* (Romans 1:20). Although the prodigal was wasting his substance in riotous living, he could yet reflect on, and feel the attractions of, the old homestead he had forsaken."

Adam, by disobeying God in tasting the fruit of the tree, forfeited the most blessed form of life God had given him, namely, fellowship with Himself. *"But of the tree of the knowledge of good and evil, thou shalt not eat of it: for in the day that thou eatest thereof thou shalt surely* die" (Genesis 2:17). Yet the life Adam retained imparted the capacity for him to bemoan his loss and desire its return.

The body, through which life expresses itself, is of the dust and returns to its native element: *"In the sweat of thy face shalt thou eat bread, till thou return unto the ground; for out of it wast thou taken: for dust thou art, and unto dust shalt thou return"* (Genesis 3:19). But He who brings the body to dust because of sin can raise it again from the dust in resurrection glory: *"And many of them that sleep in the dust of the earth shall awake, some to everlasting life, and some to shame and everlasting contempt"* (Daniel 12:2). *"[The Lord] shall change our vile body, that it may be fashioned like unto his glorious body, according to the working whereby he is able even to subdue all things unto himself"* (Philippians 3:21). In the New Testament, "life" is used to refer to the future life, which we now have in Christ, and which is also a gift of God:

> For the wages of sin is death; but the gift of God is eternal life through Jesus Christ our Lord. (Romans 6:23)

> And this is the will of him that sent me, that every one which seeth the Son, and believeth on him, may have everlasting life: and I will raise him up at the last day. (John 6:40)

> And I give unto them eternal life; and they shall never perish, neither shall any man pluck them out of my hand. (John 10:28)

> He that hath the Son hath life; and he that hath not the Son of God hath not life. (1 John 5:12)

This life is now hid with Christ in God: *"For ye are dead, and your life is hid with Christ in God"* (Colossians 3:3).

Another great miracle and mystery associated with the endowment of physical life is that of immortality. It is in this respect that the life of beasts differs from the life of man. When animals die, their life becomes extinct. They cease to exist. But, with man, it is not so. There is an "after death": *"And as it is appointed unto men once to die, but after this the judgment"* (Hebrews 9:27). As soon as the babe within the womb receives life, it is destined to live on forever. Whether the babe lives for a few seconds or grows up and passes the allotted span makes no difference. All receiving life from God receive its double aspect—life to be lived on earth and life, unending, in eternity. The quality of life here, and the sphere of it hereafter, depend upon a person's relationship to the Life-giver Himself. God not only supplies life, but grace and power to preserve and dedicate such a gift.

If our life here is to become a bouquet, a joy, a song—life from which all fret and fever and unbelieving anxiety have been removed—a life worth living—the life that wins, then it must be a life of full harmony with God's mind and will. A Latin proverb by the Roman philosopher Seneca expresses the sentiment of the travelers' psalm (see Psalm 90): "As is a tale, so is life: not how long it is, but how good it is, is what matters."

If life hereafter is to be one of unending bliss in the Father's home, a life destitute of sighs and sobs, regrets and remorse, a life radiant with the glory of the Lord, then there must be the assurance of eternal life here and now.

Savonarola wrote: "Every life, even the most selfish and the most frivolous, is a tragedy at last, because it ends with death." Such a philosophy, however, is only partially true. While death is the normal end of life upon the earth, "life" itself is deathless. All endowed with physical life, live forever. *"Because I live, ye shall live also"* (John 14:19).

In *The Admirable Crichton,* Sir James Barrie, the renowned Scottish novelist, makes one of his characters say, "Life, Crichton, is like a cup of tea; the more heartily we drink, the sooner we reach the dregs."

But in the life of a Christian there are *no dregs.* Dying without Christ, the sinner passes on to "dregs" in hell. For the believer, no matter how delightful life is on earth, the blend is better still in eternity. Was this not the sentiment of Robert Browning when he penned the line: "Life is probation and the earth no goal, but starting-point of man."

Unregenerate man, living only for the gratification of his selfish and sinful desires, might try to persuade himself to believe that death means oblivion. Having a good time while life lasts, he agrees with Sir John Davies, the sixteenth-century writer, "Our life is but a spark, which quickly dies." But he must be reminded that the spark of life never dies. His house of clay, abused, sin-marred and disease-ridden, perishes, but the tenant has an unending life elsewhere. Life, as a conscious existence, coming as a gift from God, carries with it His own ever-lastingness. Whether life is continued in heaven or hell, it is still a conscious existence. Death is either the gate to a richer life or to eternal death, meaning, of course, eternal separation from God.

2

THE BREVITY OF LIFE

The voices of Scripture, nature, experience, and literature are in unison when it comes to the fact of life's narrow span. In figurative language, a hymn reminds us that...

> Life at best is very brief,
> Like the falling of a leaf,
> Like the binding of a sheaf.

It also warns us that...

> Fleeting days are telling fast
> That the die will soon be cast,
> And the fatal line be passed.

From philosophers and poets we have gathered these descriptive aspects of life's brief hour. Pliny said, "Life is a vigil."

Samuel Johnson wrote,

> Catch, then, O catch the transient hours;
> Improve each moment as it flies;
> Life's a short summer—man a flower;
> He dies—alas! How soon he dies!

Shakespeare, the immortal bard, gives us the similes:

> Life is but a span....
> Life's but a walking shadow.

Adam (Lionel) Gordon gives us the verse:

> Life is mostly froth and bubble,
> Two things stand like stone—
> Kindness in another's trouble,
> Courage in your own.

John Mason Neale has taught us to sing:

> Brief life is here our portion,
> Brief sorrow, short-lived care.

From James Howell, we have the expressive couplet:

> This life at best is but an inn
> And we the passengers.

Seneca, the Latin philosopher, thought of life in these interesting ways:

> What new thing then is it for a man to die,
> whose whole life is nothing else but a journey to death?

Publilius Syrus, a Syrian writer of maxims, wrote,

> It matters not how long you have lived, but how well.

Robert Burns, the Scottish poet, would have us remember that...

Life is but a day at most,
Sprung from night, in darkness lost.

In *The Merry Wives of Windsor*, Shakespeare wrote,

Life is a shuttle.

Wordsworth speaks of those...

Whose life was like the violet, sweet,
As climbing jasmine, pure.

Burns also wrote that...

Life is all a variorum,
We regard not how it goes.

Edward Young urges us to remember that...

Life is but a chain of many deaths...
Life is the desert, life the solitude;
Death joins us to the great majority.

Thomas Hood, quaint writer of old, penned the lines:

There are daily sounds to tell us that life
Is dying, and Death is living.

The poet Longfellow has this sentiment:

Our little life is but a gust
That bends the branches of thy tree,
And trails its blossoms in the dust.

Sir John Davies speaks of the brevity of life thus:

Our life is but a spark, which quickly dies.

It is to Edward Fitzgerald we owe these beautiful lines:

> The Wine of life keeps oozing drop by drop,
> The Leaves of life keep falling one by one.

A Greek proverb has it:

> Life is a wheel, and good fortune is unstable.

Robert Browning stated that…

> Life is probation, and the earth no goal,
> But the starting point of man.

Carlyle tells us that…

> Life…is a poem.

Thomas Carlyle also viewed life in the same way:

> He who would write heroic poems must make his whole life a
> heroic poem.

It is to the Bible, however, we must turn for the most forceful figures of speech regarding life's little hour. God's incomparable Word views life in many ways. The emblems it uses suggest speed or flight.

Psalm 90 is adorned with a variety of figures all expressive of the quickness with which life passes. It vanishes *"as a watch in the night,"* signifying one short spell in the bivouac of the generations as they camp out in the open field of time. Life is *"as…a flood,"* as suddenly, swiftly flooding, rapidly falling mountain torrents, Moses often witnessed. It is also *"as a sleep,"* soon over and during which we are unconscious of time. Again, it is *"as withering grass,"* now green and flourishing but soon blighted and withered. Life passes *"as a tale that is told"* and over *"like a sigh."*

> Out, out, brief candle!
> Life's but a walking shadow, a poor player,
> That struts and frets his hour upon the stage,
> And then is heard no more.
> It is a tale told by an idiot, full of sound and fury,

Signifying nothing.

(*Macbeth* Act 5, scene 5, 19–28)

Life is likewise likened unto a "fading leaf," the flying "weaver's shuttle," vanishing "vapor." With all of these reminders of life's brevity, what else should we do but number our days and apply our hearts unto heavenly wisdom? May "the *rest* of our time" be used to ascertain and accomplish the will of God. (See 1 Peter 4:2.)

How sacred should that one life ever be,
That narrow span!

If, like Blacklock, we view life as "a bumper filled by fate," then, whether it be short or long, it will result in no joy to ourselves, no blessing to others, no glory to God. Robert Murray McCheyne's candle of life was snuffed out at the early age of twenty-eight. But into his short years he packed eternal results. His brief life was a "bumper" filled with a passion for God and for the souls of men. He once wrote:

I would be missed when gone;
I would not—my life done—
Have no eyes wet for me,
No hearts touched tenderly,
No good of me confessed;
Dead—and yet not missed.

King Jehoram did not live so very long. What days were his were worthless, for we are told that he "departed without being desired." Brief life can yet be blessed. But there is some truth in Thomas Carlyle's saying that "a well-written life is almost as rare as a well-spent one." Says old Walter Watson, "As we journey through life, let us live by the way."

How brief was the earthly life of Jesus! He was "dead before His prime," but He lived by the way. His constant delight was to do the will of Him who gave Him physical life.

We know not when we are to reach the end of life's road. The God who gave us life is "the length of our days," and is the only One who can enable us to live nobly by the way. If life is but a tale, let it be a story well told—a story with clean, unspoiled pages. If life is a story of charm, then ours will not be the expressed regret of Robert Burns:

> O Life! thou art a galling load,
> Along a rough, a weary road,
> To wretches such as I.

Satan, although the father of lies, lighted for once upon the truth when he said, *"All that a man hath will he give for his life"* (Job 2:4). The underlying thought being that a man will give anything or everything for life, seeing he loves it. Such a love is universal, although there are times in almost every life when hope fades—hours of depression; hours of unutterable anguish and melancholy; hours when one is half in love with easeful death. Suicide, however, is abnormal. The pauper clings to his life as grimly as the prince in his palace. Our individual life was given us to retain, and, with all its tangle and tears, is a rich heritage from God.

For Christ, life, although brief, meant character. To Him, its sum total was not merely eating, drinking, and working. He taught that a man's life does not consist in the abundance of things possessed. Life is not a playground, but a school in which we are equipped for a larger life beyond. If, however, we would experience the love of life, it is essential to live the life of love.

Too many of us conduct our life, even if we journey beyond the three-score years and ten, on the *cafeteria* plan, *self-service* only. It was not so with Lloyd Jensen, whom I met several years ago, and the sight of whom I will never forget. Shown into a room of indescribable anguish, I yet wrote of it at the time as "Sunshine Corner." Never will I cease to praise God for all that visit meant to my soul. Lloyd Jensen, one of God's heroes, had discovered the art of turning a bed of pain into one of the brightest spots on earth. Healthy and active for the first twelve years of his life, at the age of thirteen a mysterious illness overtook him, which was ultimately diagnosed as the worst form of arthritis, and which developed into Still's disease—a fearful malady resulting in the hardening of the members of the body. For over eleven years Lloyd had lain in one position on his back. During the last six years of his life this hero was practically helpless and could not move any part of his emaciated frame. All his joints were set. His hands, corrupt and distorted, rested upon a pillow of soft cotton wool. Exposed, these rock-like, ugly lumps had been fixed upon his chest for almost six years. His legs and feet were gruesome to behold. Lloyd could not open his mouth beyond the width of a cracker, yet it was in this way that his patient, devoted mother fed him small pieces of food.

When he first took sick, Lloyd was not a Christian. His young heart was somewhat rebellious at being kept in bed when others of his age could walk and play. The prayers of a godly mother prevailed, however, and through the influence of a gospel radio program Lloyd became a born-again soul. Afflicted though he was, he yet determined to read the Bible through. He felt that shame would be his if he met his Lord without having meditated upon His Word from cover to cover. His Bible rested upon a small music stand and with his head half turned, its only position night and day for years, he read the open pages, his dear mother turning those pages for him.

Of his sufferings, Lloyd had nothing to say. If visitors came to sympathize, they quickly expended it upon themselves for having grumbled over little troubles and ailments. To all who entered his room, Lloyd smilingly testified of a Savior's love. He had learned to live his life—and what a life—effectively. Lloyd has been with the Lord for many years now, but he still speaks to my heart of glorious triumph over unspeakable anguish.

As the shadows of judgment are gathering around this guilty world, the day of grace will soon end for us, whether we are at the springtime, summer, or winter of life. May wisdom be ours to sit loose to things of earth and to live each day as if it were to be our last on earth! If the days of our life are lived as under our heavenly Taskmaster's eye, then, as they come and go, no regrets will be ours.

When our life's work is ended, we will have left behind us footprints on the sands of time.

3

THE TRUST OF LIFE

To man has been committed no trust so sacred as that of life. Too many betray such trust! Life is a priceless capital, and it is tragic when it is wasted in unprofitable investments. The question each of us must face, then, is what will I do with my life? Irrespective of its length, it will be either a channel of untold blessing to others or an avenue of pernicious influence. It is not the length of life that tells, but the quality of it.

God did not bestow such a gift upon us for the sole purpose of making our narrow span as bearable and pleasurable as possible. As the divine Potter, He molded body and life together and had a set plan in our birth. We are not in the world as the result of fate or blind chance, but by divine choice. We are here to translate God's will and Word into life; and the loving, planning, all-wise God is ever with us, imparting grace and power for the realization of His purpose in our individual life.

Because God gave us life, He has every claim to it. We only court disaster if we try to live our life apart from Him. All that is twisted, sorrowful, and sinful in life, whether it be individual or collective, is the result of living without God.

Paul had no uncertainty about his ambition. *"For to me to live is Christ"* (Philippians 1:21). For to me to live is—that which follows *is*, shapes the manner of our present life, and determines the quality of our life to come.

For to me to live is—the gratification of selfish and sinful desires. I am content to eat and drink while life lasts, for tomorrow I die. All who share this aspect of life are dead as they live.

For me to live is—the participation in the pleasure and pursuits of the world. While I am alive, I must see life and enjoy myself. My time and money must further my personal happiness and contentment. But the life of self is death. Only the death of self is true life.

For to me to live is—indulgence in crime, matching my wits against organized society. When we think of the growing army of criminals who are parasites in society, living on what they can extort or steal from others, we realize how many there are who prostitute their gift of life.

For to me to live is—prestige, influence, honor, social advantages, and eminence in society. The rich young ruler our Lord spoke of had many desirable advantages, but he had to be told that he lacked the most important thing in life.

What bitter disillusionment, boredom, emptiness, and barrenness are ours when the capital of life is squandered. When Christ is not our life, we only exist. Nobility of life does not depend upon external surroundings and trappings, material affluence, social or political influence, robust health, carnal indulgences, or cultural attainments. It comes as the result of blissful harmony with the will of Him—the Giver of life. And when we live as those "alive from the dead," and as unto Him who died and rose again on our behalf, then ours is life indeed.

For none of us liveth to himself, and no man dieth to himself. For whether we live, we live unto the Lord; and whether we die, we die

unto the Lord: whether we live therefore, or die, we are the Lord's.
(Romans 14: 7–8)

But that with all boldness, as always, so now also Christ shall be magnified in my body, whether it be by life, or by death. For to me to live is Christ, and to die is gain.   (Philippians 1:20–21)

It is both interesting and profitable to note how philosophers and poets have described the precious gift of life, which Cicero exhorts us to "regulate wisely."

Sir James Barrie, in *The Little Minister*, wrote of life as "a long lesson in humility." No matter how long some people live, they never seem to learn such a lesson.

Oliver Wendell Holmes, in *The Professor at the Breakfast Table*, would have us think of life as "a great bundle of little things." But is it not made up of a good many big things as well?

Tennyson spoke of "a life that leads melodious days." This poet of the heart also gave us the lines:

Love took up the harp of Life,
And smote on all the chords with might.

Shakespeare likewise wrote of "the music of men's lives." Can we say that ours is a life without any discord? When fully possessed by and for the Lord, the days of life become "vibrant with the melody and music of heaven." The "daily beauty is his life," which Shakespeare speaks of in *Othello*, becomes ours.

The figure of life as a dream is common to many writers. Robert Burns, the Scottish poet, penned the line "life and love are all a dream." A Spanish proverb reads, "Life is a dream." From Longfellow, we have the couplet:

Tell me not, in mournful numbers,
Life is but an empty dream!

Longfellow also wrote that "Life is real! Life is earnest!" And so it is.

George Borrow philosophizes thus:

> Life is very sweet, brother, who would wish to die?...
> At last awake
> From life, that insane dream we take.

Poets, however, may write of life as if it was a dream, but the stark reality of life is the experience of multitudes that live. It is no dream in these days of sin, sickness and sorrow, want, wantonness and war, to live godly in Christ Jesus. The life of man on earth is a grim warfare against satanic forces bent on robbing lives of all that wins and is winsome and of the life more abundant. While Elizabeth Browning refers to the fact that "a quiet life, which was not life at all," was hers, there is a serenity of soul even amid storms that Jesus can make possible for His saints. May we be among the number Walter Savage Landor, eighteenth-century philosopher, described: "who warm both hands before the fire of life!"

Believing that life is ours to use for the Giver, we will be saved from its misuse. Regulating life wisely, we will agree with Cicero that "Nature has given us life, at interest, like money, no day being fixed for its return." A full understanding of the purpose of life will prevent us from the pitfalls Longfellow expressed in the lines:

> Oh, thou child of many prayers!
> Life hath quicksands, Life hath snares!

Philip Massinger, a sixteenth-century poet, reminds us that

> This life's a fort committed to my trust,
> Which I must not yield up till it be forced,
> Nor will I.

Some there are who seem to have a grudge against life. As they journey through it, they do not live by the way.

In *Epistle to a Young Friend*, Robert Burns wrote, in 1786:

> O Life! how pleasant is thy morning,
> Young Fancy's rays the hills adorning!

> Cold-pausing Caution's lesson scorning,
> We frisk away,
> Like schoolboys at th' expected warning,
> To joy and play.

To those, however, who live their life nobly and well, its sunset hours can be as pleasant, if not pleasanter, than its morning hours.

Shakespeare, in *King John*, described the attitude of many who believe that

> Life is as tedious as a twice- told tale.
> Vexing the dull ear of a drowsy man.

He also wrote in *All's Well that Ends Well* that "the web of our life is of a mingled yarn, good and ill together."

Alexander Pope, who reminded us that "on life's vast ocean diversely we sail," held a somewhat gloomy view of his own voyage, for he also wrote of "This long disease, my life." It is to be hoped that this is not our estimation of our brief span. If we can truly sing with Frances Ridley Havergal:

> Take my life and let it be
> Consecrated, Lord, to Thee,

Then, we will not be among the number Sir William Watson describes so vividly who

> Stammered and stumbled, and the wrong parts played
> And life a Tragedy of Errors made.

Shakespeare, in *Macbeth*, referred to those who throw their life away, treating it as "'twere a careless trifle." A life without Christ is a lost life. He alone, who gave His life for our sins, can give to our life zest and purpose and nobility. If we...

> Live for self we live in vain,
> If we live for Christ, we live again.

John Gay, of the seventeenth century, in *My Own Epitaph*, spoke of his misspent life in these lines:

> Life is a jest; and all things show it,
> I thought so once; and now I know it.

But as Thomas Hood, in *The Sea Spell*, expressed it:

> Their pangs must be extreme,—
> Woe, woe, unutterable woe,—
> Who spill life's sacred stream!

4

THE DEDICATION OF LIFE

Have you ever asked yourself the question, "What do I want most out of life?" If you had an Aladdin's lamp, what would you wish for first? Probing your dreams, aspirations, and ambitions, what desirable thing occupies the preeminent place? Too many want nothing more than "the life of Riley," with liberty and leisure to do exactly as they please. They seek freedom from all harassing cares and responsibilities. They strive to get away from the humdrum tedium of daily existence. They give themselves to the accumulation of enough money to provide contentment and a good time in pleasure of travel.

All too few give attention to the fact that a satisfying, religious faith and witness are the most important aspects of life. Preoccupation with material things blinds man to the vital need of greater spiritual resources. The majority are "too busy getting bread and butter, with a little jam, to gather sustenance for the inner life." It is not until spiritual hunger pains become distressingly acute that a man views life as a trust from God, to be used for His glory. There is a segment of society with no desire to live. In his anguish, Job cried, "*My life. I loath it; I would not live alway*" (Job 7:15–16). David wished, "*Oh that I had wings like a dove! For then would I fly away, and be at rest*" (Psalm 55:6). Theirs is the sentiment of the Latin proverb that says, "Life is nothing else but a journey to death." But, as Philip Massinger puts it, "There are a thousand doors to life."

In this somewhat longer chapter, we want to draw attention to some of these doors to life through which, if we pass, we can live effectively. Upon his deathbed, Augustus Caesar asked whether he had "well played his part in the comedy of life." And those for whom this book is meant can have the assurance that they have well-played their part, if they serve God in any of the ways suggested.

As they serve, they will not fail to bear in mind that God alone can answer the Muslim's prayer on their behalf, "Give me a death in which there is no life, and then a life in which there is not death"—a death to sin, a life to God.

Returning to the promise indicated in our preface, that the aim in this volume is to guide Christians in the effective use of their spare or leisure time, that is, the time they have on their hands once their vocational hours have ended, it may prove profitable to consider, first of all, this whole question of leisure.

5

EFFECTIVE USE OF LEISURE

We are not going to discuss how the worldling employs his off-time. It is clearly evident that too many people whose lives are lived independently of God, and of His claims upon their time, use such a treasure as they deem best. For the true Christian, all leisure time will bear the imprint of *Christian*. Spare hours will be employed effectively for the glory of the Master, as well as for one's own spiritual profit, and the lasting benefit of others.

The period of our off-time is one of gravest peril, for, whether we be saint or sinner, the axiom is true that "Satan finds some mischief for idle hands to do." It is a somewhat striking fact that the majority of crimes are committed during off hours, when physical energy is unleashed. Cowper wrote expressively, "Man deals with life as children with their play, who first misuse, then cast their toys away."

The dictionary describes *leisure* as being "freedom afforded by exemption from occupation or business—time free from employment." J. B. Watson, editor of *The Witness*, England, says: "Leisure is the unmortgaged remnant of our time, the fraction that is left over after all obligations have been met and duties done."

All of us are aware that modern civilization has provided us with a good deal of leisure. Labor unions have striven for a forty-hour work-week, and the majority of toilers give eight hours a day, five days a week, to their salaried employment. As there are 168 hours in a week, if we sleep on an average of eight hours a night, we are left with seventy-two hours to use profitably, or to abuse. And a person's use of his leisure declares whether his desires are regulated by selfish and sinful principles or by spiritual aspirations. Far too many of us are guilty of calculated murder! *We kill time.* We forget it is a precious commodity, to be redeemed or bought up. We have not learned the secret of getting twenty-four hours worth of living *per diem*.

Joseph T. Shipley, in his fascinating volume *The Dictionary of Word Origins*, reminds us that leisure is from the Latin word *licere*, meaning "to be permitted," that is, permitted to refrain from giving service. One that thus refrains is probably *lazy*, but *lazy is* just a shortening of *layserly* or *leisurely*.

It is from *licere* that we have the English word *license*, meaning permission or freedom. Since this was frequently carried too far, there came very soon the meaning held, also, in the adjective *licentious*. A *licentiate* was a friar authorized to hear confessions, then the person granted a University *license* to practice a profession. In their modern usage of the words *leisure*, *lazy*, and *license* are word-cousins. In the modern usage of these words, too many people destroy their leisure hours with too much laziness or licentiousness.

Jesus recognized the need of leisure. This was why He called His disciples to come apart and rest awhile. He knew that if they did not come apart they would soon fall apart! People go to pieces simply because they make no provision for peaceful leisure hours. Christ, once a carpenter, knew that labor and leisure make up life for us all. Thus, He calls us to Himself for rest. Some are all labor and little leisure, with over long hours stunting the growth of mind and spirit. Business pressure leaves them dead tired at the end of the day, with no time no inclination for a newspaper, a book, or a pleasant diversion. We have met those who are so greedy for work, and who openly boast they never take a holiday. If they only knew it, such deluded souls are only ordering their coffin in advance.

In his illuminating study *Early Christianity*, Dean Farrar tells the story of a young man who travelled to see the aged apostle John. When at last he was ushered into the presence of the disciple Jesus loved, his face registered disappointment, for John, instead of being wrapped in meditation or engaged in prayer, was playing with a pet partridge. The old man was quick to discern the look on his young visitor's face, and pointed to a bow standing in the corner of the room. "Notice, friend," he said, "that the bowstring is released. It is needful to relax at times, otherwise the bow would become useless through continual tension." So with the human spirit and body—they need to be relaxed from tension at times in order to retain their powers. And what is leisure? Is it not "release from tension in order to renew resilience"?

Several years ago, while living in Liverpool, I was impressed by the newspaper account of a tragedy overtaking an eminent business man, who after retiring from business at an early age, committed suicide because he "had nothing to do." Thomas John Hughes, at the early age of twenty-two, founded the renowned outfitters establishment known as J. T. Hughes & Company. He started out with a small shop and five helpers. When he retired at forty-two, there was a large establishment with a staff of over 700. To achieve his enormous results and success, Mr. Hughes gave himself no rest from business for twenty years. It was his whole life. He had no time for hobbies or pleasure. He was never known to take a vacation. His was a single-track mind, its destination the success of his business. Great prosperity came to him, and at forty-two he retired, a very wealthy man. But what happened? His immense energies were stilled. His active brain, no longer occupied with the details of business, had no other interest in his life. Richly able to enjoy life, he now had nothing to do. His end came suddenly. On a sea voyage, he shot himself, dropped into the sea, and was never recovered. His closest friends testified that death was due to the misery of mind he often expressed at having nothing to occupy himself with. He found himself with leisure he did not know how to use.

Medical files abound in tragic stories of those who never cultivated an alternative interest. They lived and labored hard without ever learning how to endure their own society. Morbid and suicidal tendencies in the lives of those who face complete idleness are well known to doctors and psychologists. Here is the way medical authorizes express this danger: "If a man, after many years of active life, becomes completely idle, his brain muscles and all the organs of the body stagnate, and waste products poison them.

"This results in a loss of the sense of well-being, melancholy, and an exaggeration of all the little pains and bodily discomforts which one has not time to attend to or worry about when at work.

"One or more interesting hobbies are, in fact, absolutely necessary at this time to prevent rapid degeneration of the brain. The more active the life, the greater the need of a hobby.

"It should be one that gives as much interest as the lifework did, and the wise man will begin to cultivate it for some years before his probable retirement."

On the other hand, there are those who find themselves dominated by a passion for leisure and pleasure. Pastimes, and not work, are their first consideration. Too many children of wealthy parents are in this category. They are strangers to an honest day's work in their dissipated life.

It is unnecessary to prove that there is a right and a wrong use of leisure. What we call *leisure*, namely, freedom from occupational responsibilities, is not mere idleness but a change of interests. Idle, purposeless hours are to be dreaded and guarded against.

> Principalities and powers,
> Mustering their unseen array,
> Wait for thy unguarded hours,
> Watch and pray.

General fitness depends upon the effective use we make of our spare time. Mental and moral deficiency follows on the heels of wasted free hours. Years ago, while working in the Woolwich Arsenal, I noticed that some men returned to work on Monday thoroughly exhausted because of the demoralizing ways in which they had used their weekend of rest. They knew how to employ themselves to good account during their stated working hours. They were trained and disciplined to work well—the foreman saw to that! But away from all restraints, it was another story.

We have schools to teach students to do all kinds of things, but no courses to train them how to use their spare time—so they employ or waste it as they deem fit. They have no one standing by them to rebuke them for misspent leisure. They treat it as they would never dare to treat their daily tasks. We hear a great deal about the dignity of labor, but why do we not teach people that there is such a thing as "the dignity of leisure"? Jeremy Taylor, in *The Care of Time*, reminds us that the right use of our time has a lot to do with holy living.

Christians, of course, have learned that discipline and diligence in leisure produce pleasure and profit. A Christian that is diligent in leisure, as well as in business, is one whose life counts for God in a world of need. The majority of those who trained themselves for the highest honors, never frittered away their off hours. Noble souls like William Carey and David Livingstone prepared themselves to walk with princes by employing their leisure for self-education. Much midnight oil made them the shining lights they ultimately became.

The great evangelist D. L. Moody, long before he became famous and while yet he was earning his living as a salesman, was busy for the Master in his spare time. One of his activities, and one which could be copied by many others today, was to rent four pews in church, and then go out into the streets to collect people to fill the vacant seats. Dr. Barnardo, before he became a doctor and long before he became known as the friend of outcast children, gave his spare time to searching out the poor, homeless waifs of the city.

In fact, the annals of Christian service show that as much, if not more real service for Christ is done by those who can only spend their spare time, rather than by those who give their full time to the work of the church. Think of the huge army of voluntary, spare-time preachers—men and women who not only preach on Sunday, but who give their evenings to the preparation of their sermons. Think of the large number of tract-distributors, of open-air speakers, of leaders and helpers in work among women and children, the sick and distressed. Think of those who regularly visit hospitals and lodging houses, who sing in church choirs. The Sunday school teachers must not be forgotten in this connection, nor those who work among youth in the many and varied organizations which rally the young people for God and the church.

But the work of God sadly needs more workers. Hugh Redwood, in one of his parables, said that God wanted less architects and more bricklayers—He wants more of both. He certainly wants more who will put originality and enterprise into their service for God.

The Christian churches in a certain American city were becoming alarmed at the progress of a certain political faction. They found that an army of volunteer workers rose at 5 AM every Sunday to insert a propaganda leaflet in the newspapers left on doorsteps. It is to be questioned whether the churches could raise such an army!

It is nevertheless true that many humble followers of Christ sacrifice, in lowly service for the Master, their spare time, which might be spent in recreation or an interesting hobby.

One young woman, who used shorthand in her daily work, used to take down the evening sermon in church and transcribe it for her aged grandmother, who was deaf, so she might have it to read and ponder. She then heard of another old lady who was deaf, so she typed out the sermon and made copies. Then her number of deaf and infirm friends grew until she used to visit one who read the sermon early in the week, to take it on to another. At last her work became an extensive ministry, to which most of her time was given. Truly a Christlike service!

A dear old gentleman, who always looked the picture of Christian joy, set out to win the young men of his neighborhood for Christ. Whenever he met any youth in the street, he would engage him in conversation and pass on a little book, especially written for boys. Many a young man was kept straight in critical years by the kindly interest of this humble old Christian.

A woman, denied the joys of motherhood herself, used to seek out some poor mothers with several small children and spend her one free afternoon in visiting them. When she had won their confidence, she offered to watch the children, while the mother went to service on Sunday evening. When she wanted to extend her activities, she enlisted the aid of other women who were ready to sacrifice their Sunday evenings at church for the same good cause.

A postman in Edinburgh, now gone to glory, carried on a ministry for God among his colleagues for many years. He obtained permission from his superior officer to see the sick list every week, and made it his business to go either to the home or to the hospital of every sick colleague. He would always take with him some little treat, paid for out of his own wages, and leave some printed message behind him, besides ministering cheer and comfort during his visit. God blessed his simple ministry to many souls.

The world full of troubled and needy souls is a fruitful field for sacrificial service. Do you spend your spare time, your leisure hours, for God?

Several years ago the *New York Times* carried a brief article on how some great men used their leisure:

Mendel raised sweet peas in the little time unclaimed by his monastic duties, and, by study of their variations, discovered the laws which control heredity in plants and animals. Priestley, who was a dissenting clergyman, tried chemical experiments in his small leisure, and discovered oxygen. A Liverpool longshoreman in his off hours gained distinction as a microscopist. A. Lawrence Rotch devoted his leisure to flying kites which carried recording instruments and presently he knew more about conditions in the upper air. Bently in Vermont gained an international reputation by disclosing in photo-micrographs the intricate structure and amazing, varied beauty of snowflakes.

These are, of course, exceptional cases, but next to unemployment, the most pressing question is: "What are we going to do with our increasing leisure? Waste it or use it to our highest personal development?"

In a very telling fashion, J. B. Watson informs us that, negatively, our leisure should never be spent on:

- Anything that vitiates taste for spiritual things. Particularly we should watch our reading.

- That which develops distaste for daily duty, a spirit of rebellion or contempt for it; the search for thrills, sensations, and the like.

- That which destroys our separation from evil things, such as excursions into worldly associations.

- That which takes us where our Christian testimony is compromised. Beware of borderline things, and if in doubt, leave it alone. Ask, "Is it lawful? Is it expedient? Is it enslaving?"

God gives us leisure as "a pause that refreshes." By the right exercise of it we refit ourselves for the stern realities of life. Spent powers are re-created and refitted for regular and responsible labors. Through the ministry of renewal we are energized, spiritually and mentally, for all our occupation demands of us. To quote Editor Watson again: "In the succession of our days, which are like a weaver's shuttle, we are weaving our own glory robes. The white linen is the righteous acts of the saints."

If our leisure is to fulfill its function, one or two necessary principles must be rigidly observed. For instance:

It should be re-creative. Recreation simply means to re-create or restore the energy or nerve power drained by mental or physical labor. If our leisure does not recreate, then its wrong use enervates or weakens our nerve force. Leisure, therefore, is only profitable when it is used to increase our capital and more perfectly fit us for life's responsibilities.

It should be restful. If the day's task has been heavy and taxing, then *rest* is essential. Both men and machines work better after a rest. And by rest we do not imply mere idleness, for Satan still finds mischief for idle hands to do. A change of interest is necessary to lift our thoughts from the care and concern of our daily task. Leisure, then, is only beneficial when it is looked upon as a temporary swing from the familiar to the unfamiliar. At eventide, Isaac arose and went out into the fields to meditate. Some turn to relaxing hobbies that never tire, but rather rest and invigorate them.

It should be educative. There is no need to be dependent upon created, artificial amusements for a change. Too many use their free time for participation in exhausting, worldly pleasures and pursuits. They forget that "a good man is satisfied in himself," and one can find delight and inspiration in one's off hours in good books, innocent pastimes, and in nature herself. Such pastimes are not a mere passing of time—a wanton waste of a God-given commodity. The Christian above all others is one who must give to every flying minute something to keep in store. At the judgment seat of Christ, an account will have to be given of the use of our time, as well as our talents.

It should be all-inclusive. Paul reminds us that at the center and circumference of all we do, there must be the glory of God. "*Whether therefore ye eat, or drink, or whatsoever ye do, do all to the glory of God*" (1 Corinthians 10:31). Here then, is the final law determining the right employment of our time, whether we are at labor or leisure. "All" immediately cuts out habits and pleasures many engage in when they are free. There is much grandeur in the sweeping universality of the apostolic rule which implies all life and every act of life must be consecrated by holy motives. Life is not cut up into sections, with some parts we call spiritual and other parts secular. Everything a Christian does should be Christian.

Too often young people especially are guided by *questions* rather than by *principles*. Is there any harm in this? Should I do that? Should I go there? They forget time is not their own, something with which they can do as they like. The principle laid down by Paul delivers one from all miserable, self-seeking, carnal, degrading pleasures, and lifts us out of the murky atmosphere of earth into the serene air of heaven itself. As creatures, we should live as unto the Creator. All we have and are belongs to God and should be used for the pleasure and profit of God, as well as ourselves.

Robert Murray McCheyne had inscribed upon the face of his watch, to remind him of the seriousness and brevity of life, "The night cometh!" For each of us, whether at work or at rest and play, the prayer should ever rise:

> Take my moments and my days,
> Let them flow in ceaseless praise.

6

THE EFFECTIVE WORKER

The worker is much bigger than his work. Failure to remember such a fact results in lack of efficiency. Certainly, right tools are necessary for without them there can never be any merited effectiveness. But in Christian work, the worker must take heed unto himself. Preparation of himself determines the quality of service rendered.

Beneficial service can only spring from a life hid in God. He does not seek the service of any whose hearts are destitute of His grace. Regeneration is the basis of true and effective labor for the Master. Without such a foundation, work for Him becomes mere drudgery. If one is bent on witnessing to others of a Savior's grace, he must have first-hand knowledge of what He can do for one, otherwise any phase of witness will be without effect. The worker must also keep fresh in his soul and alive in his memory the experience of his surrender to God. The fresh, vivid realization of the pit from which he was taken will keep him in touch with those as needy as he was before meeting Christ, and will also exercise a separating influence over his life. The ever-fresh remembrance of a personal salvation prevents service from becoming an irksome treadmill.

In the next place, the worker, whether clerical or lay, must cultivate the consciousness of utter dependence upon the Lord. Without Him, the worker is, and can do, nothing. Wise methods, arduous toil, and prolonged effort accomplish nothing if one is cut off from the divine source of supply. In the workday world, self-reliance is looked upon as a conquering virtue, but in Christ's service it is different. The perils of self-reliance are pitifully illustrated for us in the downfall of Samson and in the history of Uzziah. "*The Philistines be upon thee, Samson. And he awoke out of his sleep, and said, I will go out as at other times before, and shake myself. And he wist not that the LORD was departed from him*" (Judges 16:20). As for Uzziah, "*his name spread far abroad; for he was marvelously helped, till he was strong. But when he was strong, his heart was lifted up to his destruction: for he transgressed against the LORD his God*" (2 Chronicles 26:15–16). Distrust in self is the condition of effectiveness and victory. Christ, who is our grandest Model, has in this particular left us an example. He worked so incessantly yet lived near to the heart of His Father. Martin Luther used to say, "I have so much work to do today that I must find time for more prayer." All who would effectively work must persistently pray. Prayer has been spoken of as "the forgotten secret of the Church." Each of us must realize that lack of prayer-passion means the loss of vital power.

An ever-deepening and undying love for Christ is another avenue of effective service. He is more concerned about our love than our labor for Him. "Lovest thou Me?" Such a warm love regulates conduct, restrains natural inclinations, leads to obedience, and creates blessedness. The Ephesian church had many excellent qualities but was lacking in the essential quality of love. (See Revelation 2:1–7.) The Christian worker must ever be on his guard against losing his personal love to Christ. If he would keep such a love alive within his heart he must—

+ Abstain from all appearance of evil.
+ Refrain from the cold air of irreligious company. Avoid the act about the propriety of which there is doubt.

✦ Be careful not to allow lawful things to gain the ascendancy.

Further, the worker will recognize his constant need of the Spirit's unction. After all, it is not our work that counts, but the Spirit working through us. Possession of the life by, and for the Spirit, results in the endowment of power. Without His control, how ill-equipped we are to serve the Lord.

Another requisite for efficient service is the maintenance of a holy zeal and burning enthusiasm for our task. The fire must ever burn upon the altar. Spasmodic passion and ardor accomplishes little. Spirit-begotten fervor must perpetually bear us along. To keep ourselves from all chilling influences, we must constantly ponder the glorious themes of the Christian faith; meditate upon the appalling conditions of the world; enter more fully into the work of the cross; dwell upon the solemn issues of decision for Christ. It is only thus that we will find ourselves constrained to cast the whole energy of our redeemed and dedicated life into the work of God. Remembering that we are *"workers together with him"* (2 Corinthian 6:1), we come to understand the grandeur and greatness of our service and to strive to be "the best for truth and righteousness and Thee," as the invitation hymn expresses it.

7

EFFECTIVE DEDICATION

E. M. Bounds reminds us that man is looking for better methods of service, but God is looking for better men to serve. Seeing, therefore, that the worker is more important than his work—that the man himself gives weight and influence to his methods, let us go more fully into the matter of complete dedication to God. *Consecration* means the abiding condition of devotion to God and represents the dedication of all that we are and have. It entails the setting apart of our life for God, and the willingness to live all its details in reference to Him and His will concerning us. This is the basis of consecration; for once all the inner life is yielded to divine control, the outer life is not long bearing the imprint of surrender to the Master's claim.

In the first place, there must be the practical recognition of the fact, in our daily life, that if we are among those saved by grace, then we are already the Lord's. *"Ye are Christ's"*—*"We are the Lord's"* (1 Corinthians 3:23; Romans 14:8). Thus we are His, whether there is full realization of such a fact or not. Sometimes we are apt to think that the act of consecration is necessary to cause us to yield ourselves to the Lord; that henceforth we might be His, entirely and only. But the unalterable fact is that we are His. We do not become His by consecration. Consecration is undertaken seeing that we are His. "I am thine. . . Save me."

Neither does our consecration sanctify us. Faith alone in the Sanctifier can do this. Of course, there is a judicial sense in which we were sanctified as soon as we were saved. *"Ye are washed. . .sanctified"* (1 Corinthians 6:11). But what we are positionally must never be confused with what we are practically. Our *standing,* which nothing can effect, is one thing; *state* is another matter altogether. *Standing* is what we are in Christ, up in the heavenlies. *State* is what we are down here upon the earth. And the constant task of the Holy Spirit is to translate position into practice—*standing* into *state.*

Arising out of the recognition of the glorious fact that at our regeneration we are "accepted in the Beloved," comes the assurance that no matter how mixed up with mistakes and failures our dedication may be, the Lord knows our intention. The difficulty as to whether our consecration is really accepted or not, is removed. We are no longer troubled as to whether the Lord has taken us. We *have been* accepted, and as we walk in the light, the blood is able to cleanse us from all the light reveals.

The next point to emphasize is that consecration, from our side, is ever progressive. There must be the constant surrender of all that the Holy Spirit makes us conscious of. All that we know to be wrong, in the light of our present understanding of the will of God, must be yielded. And what further light may reveal regarding the doubtful things in life must be immediately abandoned. Often we are disturbed because, having given ourselves over to the Lord, we become conscious of habits and pursuits a consecrated soul should not entertain. It is then that Satan suggests that our act of consecration is not thorough. Yet it may have been, but clearer light revealed matters in a way we had not seen before. We can take fresh discoveries of our need, like these, as evidence that a real work of grace is going on within our lives. We come to see light in His light. In the Levitical offerings we have reference to the "basket of consecrations." Well, let us now deal more particularly with our basket of consecrations! What do you think the Lord expects to find in such a basket indicating the completeness of our dedication?

1. CONSECRATED BODIES

As the body is the home of the spirit and the medium of expression, as we continue in the world made up of material things, it is imperative to place this in the basket. A study of several Pauline passages convinces us of the two-fold sacredness of the believer's body. First, it must be treated with respect and care, seeing it was fashioned by God and made in His image. Second, by the incoming of the Spirit, the body has been constituted a sacred temple. Regeneration has transformed it into a mysterious cabinet of the Trinity. A dedicated body is for the Lord, and then the Lord undertakes for such a body. *"Now the body is not for fornication, but for the Lord; and the Lord for the body....For ye are bought with a price: therefore glorify God in your body, and in your spirit, which are God's"* (1 Corinthians 6:13, 20). *"I beseech you therefore, brethren, by the mercies of God, that ye present your bodies a living sacrifice, holy, acceptable unto God, which is your reasonable service"* (Romans 12:1).

Conscious of the truth that the body is His, we will not prostitute nor pervert any of its organs or powers. Habits will never be allowed to damage the utility of the body.

All questions relative to eating, drinking, dress, rest, paint, and tobacco, find a solution when the body bears the stamp of consecration to God.

2. CONSECRATED TALENTS

We read of the Nazarite that *"the consecration of his God is upon his head"* (Numbers 6:7), which means that his uncut hair was a symbol of the purity and devotion of his profession. As the head, however, represents the seat of intelligence, we come to the truth that all powers of our mind and all personal gifts and abilities must be yielded to the Lord.

Take my intellect and use
Every power as Thou shalt choose.

And, truly, the cause of Christ is waiting for the willing surrender of all the brilliant, unique gifts so many have been endowed with. The tragedy is that there are those blessed with many gifts, but with so little grace. And what glory does God receive from a Christian who is all gift and no grace? On the other hand, there are those who have few gifts but who yet possess all the graces of the Spirit. Jesus, we read, came to "the place of a skull." A skull! Not much about a skull, is there? All the flesh has left it. A skull stands for emptiness, nothingness. Have we reached the place of the skull? Apart from the Lord we are, and have, nothing.

All that I am and have,
Thy gifts so free;
In joy, in grief, through life,
Dear Lord, for Thee!

3. CONSECRATED HOMES

The well-filled basket contains among its consecrations a home regulated by spiritual principles. Later on we will discuss the secret of effective homelife. The blot upon the church's record is that she gives to the world too few sanctified homes, which are ever a nation's bulwark. The home life of many professing Christians is most deplorable. And yet, one of the great secrets of a truly consecrated life is the recognition that God is just as really served by proper fulfillment of home relationships as the engagement in that which we call spiritual work.

Frequently we meet those dear souls who rebel against the constant claims of domestic life, because they seem to interfere with Christian service. But when the life of a mother or father is made up of meetings and outside activities, to the neglect of home duties, then such is a misunderstanding of what God desires. There would be fewer godless children of Christian parents, if only home had been made more fragrant with their presence. But always out and about, and consequently offering little companionship to their children, such parents are often surprised that their children grow up indifferent if not positively non-Christian.

A consecrated home corresponds to that depicted by the psalmist: *"That our sons may be as plants grown up in their youth; that our daughters may be as corner stones, polished after the similitude of a palace"* (Psalm 144:12). And in such a home there is everything conducive to contentment. Selfishness, unkindness, domestic jars, fretting, friction, and lovelessness indicate that Christ is not the Head of the home. In consecrated homes there is the control of hasty tempers, bitter words, unkind acts, and the loving discharge of those countless calls in family life angels well might envy.

There is some doggerel we used to hear children sing, part of which goes something like this:

> In the house and out of doors,
> Brushing boots and scrubbing floors,
> Washing, ironing, darning too,
> All these things we got to do.
> I'll do it all for Jesus,
> He's coming very soon.

Can you say that yours is a consecrated home? Are all its ways ordered of the Lord? Or can it be that the atmosphere of your home is positively worldly? There is little prayer within it, no family altar, no conversation taken up with the Lord and spiritual things, and the countenance of those practices and pursuits injurious to the young around. May God enable us to deposit our homes within the basket of consecration.

4. CONSECRATED COMPANIONSHIPS

If ever there was a man with everything in the basket, it was the apostle Paul. What utter devotion was his! Nothing was withheld. Without hesitation he could sing:

> My All is on the altar.

In his Corinthian letters, he makes it plain that this question of consecration covers all our companionships and partnerships and alliances. Marriage, for example, should only be in the Lord. (See 1 Corinthians 7:39.) In respect to association with unsaved people in business, secret lodges, companionships and pursuits, the injunction to *"be ye separate"* (2 Corinthians 6:14–17) is in effect.

Because of his subtlety, Satan knows how to entangle us in those partnerships apparently commendable and advantageous, but which ultimately prove disastrous to our spiritual life and progress. Can you say that all your companionships are of the Lord? As the company we keep is an index of our spiritual life, may we be found united to those who love the Lord, and who seek His pleasure. Our basket will never be complete if sanctified companionships are not in it.

5. CONSECRATED PLEASURES

As we journey on with God into deeper life, He has for His own, we are not long in discovering that every realm of life must come under His sway. And, instinctively, we come to know whether certain avenues of pleasure are acceptable or antagonistic to His will. A guiding principle we can apply to recreations, sports, reading, and amusements, is that of their spiritual helpfulness. Whatever takes us from God's House on His day dims our vision of Him, weakens our appetite for prayer and meditation upon the Scriptures, and cannot be of the Lord.

The Psalmist reminds us that *"In thy presence is fullness of joy; at thy right hand there are pleasures forevermore"* (Psalm 16:11). In Thy presence! Whatever we cannot take into His presence and ask His blessing upon, we have no right to engage in. Of this we are confident, that so many of the so-called pleasures and relaxations of religious people cannot be laid in the basket of consecration.

6. CONSECRATED BUSINESS

We find ourselves dividing life into two sections, namely, spiritual and secular. To the consecrated Christian, however, there is nothing secular. Jesus was as truly about "His Father's business" while toiling in the carpenter's shop as in the temple worshipping God (Luke 2:49). It was to those who were skilled in various crafts that the call came, *"Who then is willing to consecrate his service this day unto the Lord"* (1 Chronicles 29:5). If our work is something we cannot do to the glory of God, then no matter what profit or advantage may accrue from such, it must be sacrificed. Have you read of the godly shoemaker whose sign read, "John Smith, Shoemaker to the Glory of God"? If a Christian's daily work is pleasing to the Lord, then He can be treated as the Senior or Consulting Partner. And that He will not be a mere silent Partner many consecrated businessmen can testify, who look upon themselves as stewards, "dedicated themselves and dedicating their gains" to the maintenance of the Lord's work and workers.

A Christian in business, who desires to have his business in the basket of consecrations, will see to it that such will never rob him of the spiritual assistance to be derived from the means of grace. Neither will he be guilty of that etiquette of profession, custom of business, habits of the trade commonly recognized, but which do not bear the stamp of consecration. He will be clean, upright, transparent in all his transactions, walking worthy of God in all his dealings.

Often we hear it declared that it is impossible to be a Christian in business today. But, surely, when we argue thus we make God a liar, and His promises of no avail. The writer remembers being the guest of a stockbroker who was the cousin of Lord Haig, commander of the British forces in the First World War. We were speaking of a certain prominent business man, a Christian, who was also active on the stock exchange. Said my stockbroker friend, who made no profession of faith, "I do not believe a man can be a sincere Christian and remain on the Exchange." Well, doubtless many will disagree with such a verdict! But of this we are confident, that no professing Christian who wants God's best will resort to practices or methods which will not bear the strict investigation of God's countenance.

7. CONSECRATED MONEY

Too often the purse is the last possession to go into the basket of consecration. Under the chapter "Effective Stewardship" we deal with the subject of "tithing."

The pocket appears to take up the rear in the dedication of all we have and are! Somehow we think that we can do as we like with our money. A saint, however, has nothing of his own. "What hast thou that thou didst not receive?" Are not the silver and the gold His? Is not our money "*his Lord's money*" (Matthew 25:18)? We ask the question, "What is so-and-so worth?" But a man's true worth is to be gauged, not by the cash he possesses, but by what he used in a consecrated way for the glory of God.

Of course, no one will be negligent of his own. If he fails to make provision for dependents, Paul says that he is worse than an infidel. In the earlier days of our ministry, we were associated with a very earnest young Christian who went to extremes, and withdrew all his money from the Bank and Insurance Companies, and gave it all to Christian work. Happily he saw his folly and made his wife's future secure.

The contents of the Levitical basket typify the fatness of Christ's soul, the strength of His body, and the richness of His substance, willingly offered on our behalf. Can we say that everything is in the basket of consecration, even our substance? Why do we still cling to the gold which is to be used as road metal in heaven? There would be no debt in God's work, and certainly no retrenchment in missionary activities, if only He could have a little more consecrated money.

"Consecrations" can be translated "fillings." Martin Luther speaks of "Fill-offerings." Consecrations, then, mean hands filled. The hands of the priests were filled with parts of the ram and then waved before the Lord. And our hands are filled with one thing or another. What are yours occupied with—the world and its vanities, or Christ and His comeliness and beauty? If our hands and lives are filled full and utterly yielded to Him, who sacrificed His all for us, then nothing will be lacking in our basket of consecrations, representing, as it does, effective dedication of one's whole life.

Life fulfills the will of Him who gave it, when it proximates the passion of the apostle Paul. "To me to live is Christ." If our life is to glorify God, then it must be lived beneficially, sacrificially, and beautifully.

Dr. Alexander Smellie suggests that a five-fold presentation of a dedicated servant can be found in the New Testament. There is:

Diketes—the inwardness of service

*No servant can **serve** two masters: for either he will hate the one, and love the other; or else he will hold to the one, and despise the other. Ye cannot serve God and mammon.*   (Luke 16:13)

*And when the angel which spake unto Cornelius was departed, he called two of his household **servants**, and a devout soldier of them that waited on him continually.*   (Acts 10:7)

*Who art thou that judgest another man's **servant**? to his own master he standeth or falleth. Yea, he shall be holden up: for God is able to make him stand.*   (Romans 14:4)

Diakonos—the swiftness of service

*So those **servants** went out into the highways, and gathered together all as many as they found, both bad and good: and the wedding was furnished with guests.*   (Matthew 22:10)

*His mother saith unto the **servants**, whatsoever he saith unto you, do it….When the ruler of the feast had tasted the water that was made wine, and knew not whence it was: (but the servants who drew the water knew) the governor of the feast called the bridegroom.*
(John 2:5, 9)

Doulos—the thoroughness of service

*Paul, a **servant** of Jesus Christ, called to be an apostle, separated unto the gospel of God.* (Romans 1:1)

*Simon Peter, a **servant** and an apostle of Jesus Christ, to them that have obtained like precious faith with us through the righteousness of God and our Saviour Jesus Christ.* (2 Peter 1:1)

*The Revelation of Jesus Christ, which God gave unto him, to shew unto his **servants** things which must shortly come to pass; and he sent and signified it by his angel unto his servant John.* (Revelation 1:1)

Hyperetes—the strenuousness of service

*But Peter followed him afar off unto the high priest's palace, and went in, and sat with the **servants**, to see the end.* (Matthew 26:58)

*And Peter followed him afar off, even into the palace of the high priest: and he sat with the **servants**, and warmed himself at the fire.* (Mark 14:54)

*My kingdom is not of this world; if my kingdom were of this world, then would my **servants** fight.* (John 18:36)

Therapon—the sweetness of service

And Moses verily was faithful in all his house, as a servant, for a testimony of those things which were to be spoken after. (Hebrews 3:5)

The fully dedicated worker is also a witness, that is, one who tells out what he knows: *"But ye shall receive power, after that the Holy Ghost is come upon you: and ye shall be witnesses unto me both in Jerusalem, and in all Judaea, and in Samaria, and unto the uttermost part of the earth"* (Acts 1:8).

He is likewise an ambassador: *"For which I am an ambassador in bonds: that therein I may speak boldly, as I ought to speak"* (Ephesians 6:20).

He is a soldier: *"Thou therefore endure hardness, as a good soldier of Jesus Christ"* (2 Timothy 2:3).

He is a fisher: *"And he saith unto them, Follow me, and I will make you fishers of men"* (Matthew 4:19).

He is God's fellow-worker: *"We then, as workers together with him, beseech you also that ye receive not the grace of God in vain"* (2 Corinthians 6:1).

He is a laborer: *"For we are labourers together with God: ye are God's husbandry, ye are God's building"* (1 Corinthians 3:9).

8

EFFECTIVE BIBLE AND BOOK READING

No matter in what capacity we seek to serve the Lord, whether it is full or part-time Christian work, the worker himself must have an intimate acquaintance with the Word of God. The Bible is the efficient textbook dealing with every part of the great work to which the worker is called. No matter what profession a person may decide to enter, he must study textbooks bearing upon the sphere he has chosen. Thus it is with all who set out to serve the Lord. The Scriptures are the armory where the weapons of warfare are found, the tool chest where every necessary tool is kept. All Scripture is given unto us that we might be thoroughly furnished unto all good works: *"All scripture is given by inspiration of God, and is profitable for doctrine, for reproof, for correction, for instruction in righteousness"* (2 Timothy 3:16).

It is not within the province of this present volume to elaborate upon profitable methods of Bible study. Suffice it to say that a Bible-less worker is a useless one. Secure the inexpensive, paper-bound books, like *Methods of Bible Study* by Griffith Thomas and *Pleasure and Profit of Bible Study* by D. L. Moody, both of which are published by the Moody Press, Chicago. These two most helpful books will guide the Christian who desires to make the most of his spare time for Christ, in the field of Bible knowledge.

Among Bible helps, reference Bibles like the Scofield Bible, the Pilgrim Bible, the American Revised Version, and various editions of the Bible issued by the Oxford University Press, should be on hand. Angus's *Bible Handbook* is unsurpassed for its range of Bible information, as is also R. A. Torrey's great volume, *How to Study the Bible for Greatest Profit*. The worker desiring efficiency in his witness will not find it hard to build up a useful library of serviceable Bible helps for a small outlay.

While it is true that to the making of books there is no end, there are a few the lay worker will want to have on hand as he seeks to serve Christ efficiently. A profitable volume on Christian doctrine like the recent one published by Fleming Revell called a *Handbook on Christian Truth*, is simple, terse, and lucid, and will greatly assist the worker in presenting the truth in an orderly fashion. After D. L. Moody had been preaching for years, a friend said to the evangelist, "You have been preaching for thirty years now. Have you made any change in your sermons?" "None," was the reply, "except to make them more doctrinal."

A reliable book on Christian evidences will likewise benefit a worker as he seeks to give a reason of the hope within him. Dr. W. H. Griffith Thomas in his valuable little book *Christianity is Christ*, gives unassailable arguments for the person and work of Christ. Difficult and technical books should be avoided. Simpler volumes like *Many Infallible Proofs* by A. T. Pierson produce a full assurance of understanding *"that their hearts might be comforted, being knit together in love, and unto all riches of the full assurance of understanding, to the acknowledgement of the mystery of God, and of the Father, and of Christ"* (Colossians 2:2). These volumes produce a full assurance of faith: *"Let us draw near with a true heart in full assurance of faith, having our hearts sprinkled from an evil conscience, and our bodies washed with pure water"* (Hebrews 10:22). They also produce the full assurance of hope: *"And we desire that every one of you do shew the same diligence to the full assurance of hope unto the end"* (Hebrews 6:11).

Gathering a working library, the worker can gain much inspiration from church history. What one owes to the pioneers of our faith adds nerve to witness. The biographical form of church history makes such reading genuinely fascinating. Reasonable volumes like *Early Church History*, by Henry T. Sell; *The Church*, by J. B. Watson; *Brief History of the Christian Church*, by William Stuart, are sufficient to whet one's appetite for this form of study.

As for an accurate Bible commentary, there are three requirements to bear in mind as we set out to purchase such a Bible aid:

+ It should be explanatory of the text.

+ It should be suggestive and provocative of thought.

+ It should be truly spiritual and personal in its application.

As the majority of those who seek to serve Christ in this sphere, that is, spare-time service, do not have too much money to spend on expensive books, a thoroughly reliable set is heartily recommended, namely, *Ellicott's Commentary for English Readers*. The writer's first help along this line was good old Matthew Henry, of whom Dr. Alexander Whyte said to his students, "In him you will always get knowledge, sagacity, humor, and sometimes fun." Spurgeon said of this profitable and practical commentary, "Every minister ought to read Matthew Henry entirely and carefully through at least once."

Books containing the sermons of those God have so signally blessed also enrich one's heart and mind. For the most effective, evangelistic phraseology, live near the "sermon-ish" literature of C. H. Spurgeon, who certainly knew how to play upon the heart strings.

On books as a whole, much could be written. Because life is short, and the Christian worker eager to improve his off-hours for Christ and His service, inferior and haphazard reading must be shunned. The books he invests in must be the index of his character and passion.

While not above the use of good books in the work of the Lord, the worker will see to it that his library grows with his Spirit-enlightened mind. Of course, he will not neglect the vast and rich field of biography, biblical and secular.

Following the advice of Paul to young Timothy, "Give attention to reading," the worker is advised to avoid all books presenting false views of human life; containing a large admixture of what is coarse and evil; corrupting the imagination and arousing passions, "a reeking, and unwashed literature"; apologizing for sin and crime. Here are some profitable principles of good reading:

1. Read little that is to be immediately forgotten.

2. Read the best books. Be on speaking terms with the master-minds of the world.

3. Read the books helpful to one's mission and work.

4. Read for mental quickening. Go in for mental gymnastics.

5. Read for style, a strong and conquering speech.

6. Read for information, and store the memory with gathered facts and truths.

7. Read with pencil and notebook. Make prisoners of material you want to use.

8. Read widely. Variety of mental occupation is restful for the mind. Roam in the fields of poetry, history, romance, and science, and harness what you read, as Frank Boreham does, to the chariot of the gospel. Yes, and by the way, a well-thumbed dictionary or encyclopedia proves how one has striven to enrich his vocabulary, so that he could present the gospel more effectively. On books as a whole, we can say:

> There are treasures all round you;
> Why take the scraps, neglecting the gold?
> The great of all ages offer their treasures,
> Are you content not to see them unfold?
> They are yours if you take them, the fair gems of knowledge,

Shakespeare and Ruskin, Browning and all:
There is not a great mind of all the great ages
But silently waits to come at your call.

9

EFFECTIVE CHURCH WORK

What a difference it would make, both in the church, and to the world at large, if only all church members were active in the New Testament description of church life and work. However, the majority of churches carry too many paper-members! They are on the church roll, but not on the *roll* around the community for Christ. The heartbreak of many a godly pastor is the possession of those in his church who dissipate their energies in a round of nonessential activities, like outside clubs, lodges, social functions, sports, and pleasure that contribute absolutely nothing to the furtherance of Christ's cause in a weary, sin-cursed, blood-soaked world. How much would be accomplished for the souls of men if only the wasted hours and money could have been dedicated to the highest mission in the world! When our time off from daily occupations is spent on avenues of pleasure satisfying only to the flesh, we are simply walking on a dead-end street. All we engage in when once free of our secular tasks, at which we usually work eight hours a day, should be character-building and God-glorifying. With our livelihood taken care of, the designation of spare time should be made as unto Him who grants us life to live.

Christians associated with some form of Christian community should give to the church of their conviction and choice, the bulk of their surplus time in spiritual activities, that is, if the church adheres to New Testament standards and principles. The lamentable lack of definite Christian functions in some churches has driven many to laudable organizations like the Youth for Christ Movement, the Gideons, the Christian Business Men's committees, and similar nonaffiliated church groups, not conspicuous as antichurch in operations.

Sometimes church leaders are apt to forget that churches would cease to exist if it were not for the money people earn at their daily tasks, and in part donate to the church. Further, churches could never operate if the bulk of their membership failed to use so much of the time off from secular tasks engaged in for livelihood, to church worship and work. He is, therefore, a wise pastor who constantly strives to keep his people active and happy in the Master's business. And that there are multitudinous avenues of service, in and through the church, is testified to by scores of successful, evangelical centers over the land. The most striking example of a whole church at work for Christ is that of the Highland Park Church, Chattanooga, Tennessee, of which Dr. Lee Roberson is pastor. The amazing record of this renowned church during the last twelve years is without parallel in the denomination it represents.

As we come to discuss various branches of Christian work, it may be fitting for you, my reader, to pause and ask yourself the question, "What am I doing for the church Jesus purchased by His blood? Have I found the task in her courts I can efficiently accomplish?" If saved by grace, it is your responsibility to serve Christ, and to serve Him well. If you have undertaken to serve Christ and His church in any capacity, whether as an elder, deacon, or usher, pray that all devotion and decorum may be yours as you exercise your office.

10

EFFECTIVE CHILDREN'S WORK

This important phase of Christian service covers the Sunday school, young people's work, child evangelism, and other means of reaching those of young and tender years. No branch of service yields returns greater than this. Yet too often we set those to work among the young who are least equipped and not experienced for such a sacred task. The many agencies at work for the bringing of girls and boys to Christ testify to the importance of such a task. "We are a nation of fools," exclaimed an indignant American as he pointed to a reformatory. "Why?" he was asked. "Because we are spending such vast sums in taking care of our criminals, and so little in looking after our children!"

Work among children is always profitable work. It is much easier to win a child than an adult. It is easier for a child to believe, seeing it does not have the moral and intellectual difficulties of a grown-up. Children do not have old prejudices to overcome as adults do. "Why are your sheep so much better than your neighbors?" a farmer was asked. "Because," he replied, "I take good care of my lambs!" In these days of spreading juvenile delinquency, such a reply makes sound sense and true wisdom.

The winning of children is important from other angles. They have no evil habits to break off, no old associations to shun. If only won early for Christ, they become of much use to Him. In the salvation of a child, there is a double salvation—the soul is saved and the life is likewise saved and secured for the Master. The great Spurgeon left this testimony concerning children: "I have more confidence in the spiritual life of the children I have taken into my church than I have in the spiritual condition of the adults received. I will go further, and say I have usually found a clearer knowledge of the gospel and a warmer love to Christ in the child convert, than in the man convert." Think of it! The great Jonathan Edwards was converted at seven; Isaac Watts at nine; Robert Hall at twelve; Matthew Henry at eleven; and Spurgeon himself when a little over fifteen.

When away from your secular occupation, do you work among the young? If so, have you a desire to become more efficient in such a beneficial phase of Christian service? Well, if you are not stirred by your work you will be lacking in the devotion necessary in influencing child-life.

Roads to efficiency in child evangelism cannot be mistaken. The Bible, for instance, has a great deal to say about children and their relation to the God who gives them the great treasure of life. We note that—

Young children are capable of serving the Lord. For instance:

And the child did minister unto the LORD before Eli the priest.... But Samuel ministered before the LORD, being a child, girded with a linen ephod....And the child Samuel grew on, and was in favour both with the LORD, and also with men. (1 Samuel 2:11, 18, 26)

Josiah was eight years old when he began to reign, and he reigned thirty and one years in Jerusalem....And he did that which was right in the sight of the LORD, and walked in all the way of David

his father, and turned not aside to the right hand or to the left.
                                                    (2 Kings 22:1, 2)

But continue thou in the things which thou hast learned and hast been assured of, knowing of whom thou hast learned them; and that from a child thou hast known the holy scriptures, which are able to make thee wise unto salvation through faith which is in Christ Jesus.   (2 Timothy 3:14–15)

Young children are sometimes sanctified from their birth. About Jeremiah and John the Baptist, the Bible says:

Before I formed thee in the belly I knew thee; and before thou camest forth out of the womb I sanctified thee, and I ordained thee a prophet unto the nations.   (Jeremiah 1:5)

For he shall be great in the sight of the Lord, and shall drink neither wine nor strong drink; and he shall be filled with the Holy Ghost, even from his mother's womb.   (Luke 1:15)

Young children's security had Christ's emphasis. He says in Matthew:

And said, Verily I say unto you, Except ye be converted, and become as little children, ye shall not enter into the kingdom of heaven.... And whoso shall receive one such little child in my name receiveth me. But whoso shall offend one of these little ones which believe in me, it were better for him that a millstone were hanged about his neck, and that he were drowned in the depth of the sea....Take heed that ye despise not one of these little ones; for I say unto you, That in heaven their angels do always behold the face of my Father which is in heaven....Even so it is not the will of your Father which is in heaven, that one of these little ones should perish.
                                    (Matthew 18:3, 5–6, 10, 14)

Then were there brought unto him little children, that he should put his hands on them, and pray: and the disciples rebuked them. But Jesus said, Suffer little children, and forbid them not, to come unto me: for of such is the kingdom of heaven. And he laid his hands on them, and departed thence.   (Matthew 19:13–15)

Young children have the capacity to believe.

But whoso shall offend one of these little ones which believe in me, it were better for him that a millstone were hanged about his neck, and that he were drowned in the depth of the sea.   (Matthew 18:6)

Success in child-conversion, having the mind of God and the challenge of Christ's command, is also dependent upon the remembrance of a few simple things. For example:

+ Remember you are dealing with children, not grown-ups.
+ Remember children do not know everything.
+ Remember the older children become, the more difficult it is to win them.
+ Remember not to expect too much from children after they are won.
+ Remember to care for them after their conversion.

Efficient methods in this type of work are so necessary if the young folks, however they may be brought together under religious influences, are to find Jesus Christ. Let the following pertinent facts be borne in mind:

+ Win the love and confidence of the children.
+ Never forget the personal appeal in the lesson.
+ State the gospel truth simply and plainly.
+ Exercise patience with the more stubborn children. (A worker once said, "A boy has 500 muscles to wriggle with, and not one to sit still with.")
+ Use language the children can readily understand.
+ Adapt yourself to the ways of a child.
+ Have a thorough belief in the child's need.

+ Keep the seriousness of your task in mind.

+ Constantly rely upon the Spirit's power.

Meetings for children should always be bright, attractive, interesting, enthusiastic, and reverent. Children love to sing, so concentrate on easy, catchy choruses. Stories are likewise delighted in. No matter how gripping the story you find, be sure of its appeal for decision. A Scottish preacher tells of an experience he once had while addressing a crowd of youngsters. A heart-moving story had just been told to the group in a poor part of the city, and, at its conclusion, he said, "And now for the moral." A ragged child shouted, "Never mind the moral, guv'nor— tell us another story!" The wise worker will see to it that the point of a story is woven into the story itself. Further, never tell involved, intricate, over detailed stories. Aim to capture the interest of the youngest child before you, and your approach will be effective.

11

EFFECTIVE VACATION
BIBLE SCHOOLS

Over the years, daily summer vacation Bible schools have increased by leaps and bounds. The majority of denominational and nondenominational churches have come to realize their value, and, as summer vacation from secular education rolls around, opportunity is taken of capturing the interest of the young for spiritual ends. Christian day-school and Sunday school teachers willingly surrender a few morning hours to capture girls and boys for Christ. And with such rapid expansion of this important phase of Christian service, there has developed literature and aids to assist those who willingly and, in the majority of cases, voluntarily give their time to this most profitable work. No other part-time ministry is more rewarding than the evangelism of the young.

The necessity of Christian child training has been created by the lamentable lack of religious instruction in home and public schools, as well as by modern psychological trends. The failure of educators to recognize the value of religious training is one of the major tragedies of our day. Our deplorable juvenile delinquency can be traced to the negligence of the spiritual welfare of the young.

The first requisite of those who form a daily vacation Bible school and labor in it is a definite experience of God's saving power within their own hearts. They cannot teach what they have never experienced. Behind all endeavors there must be a warm love for the Savior, and also for those of young and tender years they seek to win for Him.

Another personal qualification is that of self-control and endless patience. Workers will remember that they are conducting a *vacation* school, and as the youngsters are on vacation, they are apt to be restless and boisterous. Youngsters cannot be trained without respect for their teachers, and no child can ever respect a teacher who cannot control impatience. Children on vacation can be very trying, but the quiet voice, unruffled demeanor, and unhurried response to endless questions never fail to influence girls and boys who gather for the school period. Yieldedness to the Holy Spirit can produce the loving attitude, absence of quick temper, and hasty judgment so detrimental in winning the young.

Along the lines of personal preparation, mention must be made of prayer, Bible study, and the Spirit's unction. Requirements for the work we are considering are totally different from those so necessary for the teaching of secular subjects in ordinary public schools. For the fulfillment of God's commission to win the children, divine equipment is necessary. For God's interest in the religious welfare of the young, the teacher will prayerfully ponder such passages as:

> For I know him, that he will command his children and his household after him, and they shall keep the way of the Lord, to do justice and judgment; that the Lord may bring upon Abraham that which he hath spoken of him. (Genesis 18:19)

> Gather me the people together, and I will make them hear my words, that they may learn to fear me all the days that they shall live upon the earth, and that they may teach their children.... Hear, O Israel: the LORD our God is one LORD: and thou shalt

love the LORD thy God with all thine heart, and with all thy soul, and with all thy might. And these words, which I command thee this day, shall be in thine heart: ªnd thou shalt teach them diligently unto thy children, and shalt talk of them when thou sittest in thine house, and when thou walkest by the way, and when thou liest down, and when thou risest up.…When all Israel is come to appear before the LORD thy God in the place which he shall choose, thou shalt read this law before all Israel in their hearing. Gather the people together, men and women, and children, and thy stranger that is within thy gates, that they may hear, and that they may learn, and fear the LORD your God, and observe to do all the words of this law: and that their children, which have not known any thing, may hear, and learn to fear the LORD your God, as long as ye live in the land whither ye go over Jordan to possess it.

(Deuteronomy 4:10; 6:4–7; 31:11–13)

Whom shall he teach knowledge? And whom shall he make to understand doctrine? Them that are weaned from the milk, and drawn from the breasts. For precept must be upon precept, precept upon precept; line upon line, line upon line; here a little, and there a little. (Isaiah 28:9–10)

At the same time came the disciples unto Jesus, saying, Who is the greatest in the kingdom of heaven? And Jesus called a little child unto him, and set him in the midst of them, And said, Verily I say unto you, Except ye be converted, and become as little children, ye shall not enter into the kingdom of heaven. Whosoever therefore shall humble himself as this little child, the same is greatest in the kingdom of heaven. And whoso shall receive one such little child in my name receiveth me. But whoso shall offend one of these little ones which believe in me, it were better for him that a millstone were hanged about his neck, and that he were drowned in the depth of the sea. Woe unto the world because of offences! for it must needs be that offences come; but woe to that man by whom the offence cometh! Wherefore if thy hand or thy foot offend thee, cut them off, and cast them from thee: it is better for thee to enter into life halt or maimed, rather than having two hands or two feet to be cast into everlasting fire. And if thine eye offend thee, pluck it out, and cast it from thee: it is better for thee to enter into life with one eye, rather than having two eyes to be cast into hell fire. Take heed that ye despise not one of these little ones; for I say unto you, That in heaven their angels do always behold the face of my Father which is in heaven. For the Son of man is come to save that which was lost. How think ye? if a man have an hundred sheep, and one of them be gone astray, doth he not leave the ninety and nine, and goeth into the mountains, and seeketh that which is gone astray? And if so be that he find it, verily I say unto you, he rejoiceth more of that sheep, than of the ninety and nine which went not astray. Even so it is not the will of your Father which is in heaven, that one of these little ones should perish....Then were there brought unto him little children, that he should put his hands on them, and pray: and the disciples rebuked them. But Jesus said, Suffer little children, and forbid them not, to come unto me: for of such is the kingdom of heaven.

(Matthew 18:1–14; 19:13–14)

So when they had dined, Jesus saith to Simon Peter, Simon, son of Jonas, lovest thou me more than these? He saith unto him, Yea, Lord; thou knowest that I love thee. He saith unto him, Feed my lambs.   (John 21:15)

For the promise is unto you, and to your children, and to all that are afar off, even as many as the Lord our God shall call. (Acts 2:39)

And, ye fathers, provoke not your children to wrath: but bring them up in the nurture and admonition of the Lord.   (Ephesians 6:4)

Approaching the matter of effectiveness in vacation Bible school work, attention must be given to an attractive program, and attractive it must be, seeing the children voluntarily attend while on vacation. The more appealing the program, the less difficulty there will be in securing and holding the children. If the school time is characterized by warmth, action, kindly but firm discipline, and sense of a planned program, and an awareness of God, there is no fear that beneficial results will be lacking.

As to the securing of sufficient children for a vacation school, perseverance will have to be practiced in the enlistment of scholars. Children are *compelled* to go to their day school, but it is a different matter with a voluntary summer school. Among profitable methods assuring a good attendance are:

1. Personal visitation of children in the area

2. Solicitation of parents' interest in your work

Usually these summer schools are made up of churchgoing and unchurched children, which means that instruction must be directed to reach both classes. Then because various ages will be represented, a suggested grouping, herewith cited, might prove beneficial:

Kindergarten	3 to 6 years
Juniors	6 to 10 years
Seniors	10 to 15 years

For the kindergarten group, lessons must be simple. As music gives the child opportunity for expression, gospel choruses and motion songs should be used. Only those choruses should be used that have a real value. Always select those fitting in with the morning lesson. Explain the meaning of the words to the children, and lead them to understand the message of the chorus. Encourage the children to sing properly and not to shout. In the teaching of choruses, various methods can be employed:

1. Paste them on a large piece of cardboard or paper (the back of old window shades or scroll-like paper can be used).

2. Pictures can be used to visualize a chorus or hymn. Figures and scenes can be cut out of magazines for this purpose.

3. If possible, tell in simple language how the chorus came to be written or a simple incident about it.

The use and memorization of a simple Bible alphabet can also be used with effect. Verses easy to grasp should be selected. Work out the entire alphabet along this line:

a.   *"All the earth shall worship thee"* (Psalm 66:4).

b.   *"Beloved, let us love one another"* (1 John 4:7).

c.   *"Create in me a clean heart, O God"* (Psalm 51:10).

d.   *"Draw near to God and He will draw near to you"* (James 4:8 NKJV).

e.   *"Enter in at the strait gate"* (Luke 13:24).

f.   *"Fear thou not; for I am with thee"* (Isaiah 41:10).

Visual aids likewise enable the teacher to use "eye gate" in the presentation of the gospel. Learn how to draw either on a blackboard or on large sheets of white paper, with chalk or color crayons.

For the junior and senior groups, the course of instruction would be more mature, yet the simpler the better. It must be remembered at the outset that long words not in the child's vocabulary must be avoided. The presentation of the gospel and allusions to Bible lands, customs, and backgrounds must be within the realm of the young person's comprehension. Specific age groups must always be kept in mind and adaptation practiced. For example, a tiny china doll in a small basket set on a mirror enables a beginner to understand the baby Moses. For older children, however, such an object would be ludicrous.

The memorization of Bible verses should be encouraged, and never impose punishment for failure to retain the verses. Whatever the method of approach, all lessons must be Bible-centered. The teacher must handle the Bible and speak of it reverently, in order to train the young in honoring it. In teaching the Word, sometimes use the question method as Christ did in His ministry. (See Matthew 16:12–16; Luke 12:35–42.) Employ the positive and negative aspects in the use of your questions.

Positive

a.   Questions keep the interest and attention of children.

    b.   Questions stimulate their thought.

    c.   Questions can direct their thoughts to the point you are endeavoring to make.

    d.   Questions can be used in any part of the lesson.

Negative

    a.   Don't ask a question unless it pertains to the Scripture lesson.

    b.   Don't ask indefinite questions.

    c.   Don't ask tricky questions.

    d.   Don't ask questions until you have clearly explained the procedure that they must follow to answer them. If one emphasizes to the children the necessity of the class being conducted in a decent and orderly fashion they can, therefore, teach the children that by raising their hands, quietly, they will then have the opportunity to answer the question. *"Let all things be done decently and in order"* (1 Corinthians 14:40).

    e.   Don't embarrass children who haven't raised their hands by asking them questions.

A successful worker in this field says:

Children can be encouraged if they are given sufficient reasons and incentive to memorize the Word of God. They can be encouraged if we impress upon their minds not only the immediate but the future benefits that shall accrue to them if they take the time to commit to memory God's precious Word. If the teacher impresses them properly there will be little need of prizes, etc., for the memory work.

    a.   Make certain that every word in the verse is understood.

    b.   Make certain that every message in the verse is clear.

    c.   Note: Memory work is fine, but do not stop at memory work, but go on so that the child's concept of the entire verse is clear.

    d.   Teach one or two verses each lesson, and if possible one that is related to the lesson.

    e.   Repetition is a *must*.

    f.   If a child is trying to quote a verse and hesitates, don't be too quick to help him.

    g.   Make sure every word is quoted, and always give commendation for their efforts.

    h.   Construction paper cutouts with the verse or verses written upon them are helpful for home study.

    i.   Always review verses.

The skillful use of handwork also fosters deep interest in the truth, when it is correlated to the Bible. Fingers can be trained in the use of crayons, paper, and paste, and nicely decorated Scripture verses, which, when finished, can be taken home are invaluable.

As with the Kindergarten group, so with other groups, visual aids will be found practical. Scripture warrant for the use of these aids can be gathered from these sources:

STORIES FROM JEREMIAH

The broken bottle:

Thus saith the Lord, *Go and get a potter's earthen bottle, and take of the ancients of the people, and of the ancients of the priests; and go forth unto the valley of the son of Hinnom, which is by the entry of the east gate, and proclaim there the words that I shall tell thee, and say, Hear ye the word of the* Lord, *O kings of Judah, and inhabitants of Jerusalem; thus saith the* Lord *of hosts, the God of Israel; Behold, I will bring evil upon this place, the which whosoever heareth, his ears shall tingle. Because they have forsaken me, and have estranged this place, and have burned incense in it unto other gods, whom neither they nor their fathers have known, nor the kings of Judah, and have filled this place with the blood of innocents; they have built also the high places of Baal, to burn their sons with fire for burnt offerings unto Baal, which I commanded not, nor spake it, neither came it into my mind: therefore, behold, the days come, saith the LORD, that this place shall no more be called Tophet, nor The valley of the son of Hinnom, but the valley of slaughter. And I will make void the counsel of Judah and Jerusalem in this place; and I will cause them to fall by the sword before their enemies, and by the hands of them that seek their lives: and their carcases will I give to be meat for the fowls of the heaven, and for the beasts of the earth. And I will make this city desolate, and an hissing; every one that passeth thereby shall be astonished and hiss because of all the plagues thereof. And I will cause them to eat the flesh of their sons and the flesh of their daughters, and they shall eat every one the flesh of his friend in the siege and straitness, wherewith their enemies, and they that seek their lives, shall straiten them. Then shalt thou break the bottle in the sight of the men that go with thee, and shalt say unto them, thus saith the LORD of hosts; Even so will I break this people and this city, as one breaketh a potter's vessel, that cannot be made whole again: and they shall bury them in Tophet, till there be no place to bury. Thus will I do unto this place, saith the LORD, and to the inhabitants thereof, and even make this city as Tophet: and the houses of Jerusalem, and the houses of the kings of Judah, shall be defiled as the place of Tophet, because of all the houses upon whose roofs they have burned incense unto all the host of heaven, and have poured out drink offerings unto other gods. Then came Jeremiah from Tophet, whither the LORD had sent him to prophesy; and he stood in the court of the LORD's house; and said to all the people.*

(Jeremiah 19:1–14)

The yokes:

In the beginning of the reign of Jehoiakim the son of Josiah king of Judah came this word unto Jeremiah from the LORD, saying, Thus saith the LORD to me; Make thee bonds and yokes, and put them upon thy neck, And send them to the king of Edom, and to the king of Moab, and to the king of the Ammonites, and to the king of Tyrus, and to the king of Zidon, by the hand of the messengers which come to Jerusalem unto Zedekiah king of Judah; and command them to say unto their masters, Thus saith the LORD of hosts, the God of Israel; Thus shall ye say unto your masters; I have made the earth, the man and the beast that are upon the ground, by my great power and by my outstretched arm, and have given it unto whom it seemed meet unto me. And now have I given all these lands into the hand of Nebuchadnezzar the king of Babylon, my servant; and the beasts of the field have I given him also to serve him. And all nations shall serve him, and his son, and his son's son, until the very time of his land come: and then many nations and great kings shall serve themselves of him. And it shall come to pass, that the nation and kingdom which will not serve the same Nebuchadnezzar the king of Babylon, and that will not put their neck under the yoke of the king of Babylon, that nation will I punish, saith the LORD, with the sword, and with the famine, and with the pestilence, until I have consumed them by his hand. Therefore hearken not ye to your prophets, nor to your diviners, nor to your dreamers, nor to your enchanters, nor to your sorcerers, which speak unto you, saying, Ye shall not serve the king of Babylon: for they prophesy a lie unto you, to remove you far from your land; and that I should drive you out, and ye should perish. But the nations that bring their neck under the yoke of the king of Babylon, and serve him, those will I let remain still in their own land, saith the LORD; and they shall till it, and dwell therein. I spake also to Zedekiah king of Judah according to all these words, saying, Bring your necks under the yoke of the king of Babylon, and serve him and his people, and live.

(Jeremiah 27:1–12)

STORIES FROM EZEKIEL

The tile:

Thou also, son of man, take thee a tile, and lay it before thee, and pourtray upon it the city, even Jerusalem.   (Ezekiel 4:1)

The sharp knife:

And thou, son of man, take thee a sharp knife, take thee a barber's razor, and cause it to pass upon thine head and upon thy beard: then take thee balances to weigh, and divide the hair.   (Ezekiel 5:1)

STORIES OF CHRIST

The little child:

At the same time came the disciples unto Jesus, saying, Who is the greatest in the kingdom of heaven? And Jesus called a little child unto him, and set him in the midst of them, And said, Verily I say unto you, Except ye be converted, and become as little children, ye shall not enter into the kingdom of heaven. Whosoever therefore shall humble himself as this little child, the same is greatest in the kingdom of heaven. And whoso shall receive one such little child in my name receiveth me. But whoso shall offend one of these little ones which believe in me, it were better for him that a millstone were hanged about his neck, and that he were drowned in the depth of the sea. Woe unto the world because of offences! for it must needs be that offences come; but woe to that man by whom the offence cometh! Wherefore if thy hand or thy foot offend thee, cut them off, and cast them from thee: it is better for thee to enter into life halt or maimed, rather than having two hands or two feet to be cast into everlasting fire. And if thine eye offend thee, pluck it out, and cast it from thee: it is better for thee to enter into life with one eye, rather than having two eyes to be cast into hell fire. Take heed that ye despise not one of these little ones; for I say unto you, That in heaven their angels do always behold the face of my Father which is in heaven.

(Matthew 18:1–10)

Bread and wine:

And as they were eating, Jesus took bread, and blessed it, and brake it, and gave it to the disciples, and said, Take, eat; this is my body. And he took the cup, and gave thanks, and gave it to them, saying, Drink ye all of it; for this is my blood of the new testament,

which is shed for many for the remission of sins. But I say unto you,
I will not drink henceforth of this fruit of the vine, until that day
when I drink it new with you in my Father's kingdom.

(Matthew 26:26–29)

In connection with the use of visual aids, it has been computed that:

1. The eyes take in twenty-two times faster than the ears.

2. The eyes have a retention that is five times as great as the ears' retention. By such aids the children are helped to *see* the truth.

3. The average child is always arrested by properly used visual aids. Thus, when used, attention is no problem, for such objects secure both attention and retention.

Almer L. Gilleo reminds us that no matter what age level is taught, visual aids are always effective, if these simple rules are followed:

1. Select materials which are logically correlated with the lesson and make the truth clear to the students.

2. Make sure the material is suited to the age level.

3. Prepare materials well in advance and practice using them.

4. Make the visual aid a supplement in your teaching and not a substitute for the teacher.

5. Use discretion in determining what to visualize. Do not attempt to use the visual aid method for everything.

Our final word involves finances for all the equipment and supplies needed to make the daily vacation school a success. Ask God to raise you up donors in your church or mission or among your friends. Consult with your pastor and fellow Christians about your plans, seeking their prayers that every need may be met. Part of your tithe money could be used in this God-honoring work. Parents, coming to realize the usefulness of the vacation school in the lives of their dear children, will not be slow in offering financial support for the same.

12

EFFECTIVE PRAYER MEETINGS

Often in the absence of the pastor, one of the devoted laymen of a church will take over and direct the midweek service, which is always composed of faithful souls who, after the day's regular work, dedicate the evening to prayer, praise, and worship.

At the outset, a word must be said regarding the tremendous importance of the prayer meeting in the life of a church. All church members, health and circumstances permitting, should attend the weekly period for prayer and intercession. The prayer meeting is the spiritual thermometer of a church. Some time ago I was in a church with a membership of over 1,000 and a weekly attendance at the prayer meeting of only some fifteen persons. Often the prayer meeting is a misnomer. It is just another church service, with a message from the pastor or leader. But a prayer meeting should be a meeting for prayer, and little else. When will churches learn that their spiritual vitality, faith, and fervor depend upon such an "Hour of Power"? The decadence of interest in the church's prayer meeting reveals the utter prayerlessness of a church's membership. Christians believing in the power and privilege of prayer, and striving in their own personal lives to live in unbroken fellowship with God, are those who love to journey to His house to pray.

From Pentecost down there have not been spiritual awakenings in the land which did not begin in a union of praying men and women. It is also true that the decline of spiritual power in the church has been in exact proportion to the decline of desire for supplication and intercession. The church of Christ was born in a prayer meeting and her life can only be maintained by abiding in the same atmosphere. "The Acts of the Apostles," says A. T. Pierson, "is one continuous testimony to the fact and power of united prayer."

Spurgeon surely recognized the value of the prayer meeting when he said, "Brethren, we shall never so much change for the better in our character in general until the prayer meeting occupies a higher place in the esteem of the churches." Churches today are not weak in educated ministers; in beautiful, ornate, costly buildings; in form and ritual; in organizations; in good preaching. Their tragedy is that they do not pray. The generating force is missing. The late A. C. Dixon used to say that "the weekly prayer meeting is one of the best tests of Christian character." Some fifty years ago, when the writer was converted, the prayer meeting was a vital force in the church where he found the Lord, and weekly attendance at it contributed greatly to the growth of his spiritual life.

Reasons for nonattendance at prayer meetings or nonappearance at them altogether, are not hard to seek. First of all, there is a lamentable lack of desire to attend such gatherings. Where there is no heart-hunger for prayer, collective prayer is neglected. Thus, generally speaking, church members depreciate the value of a prayer meeting as a mighty force in the life and work of a church. Dinners are more important. So the supper room takes the place of the upper room. Lack of passion for souls of men is another reason for the prayer meeting's decline. When you find a church strongly evangelistic, you always discover the secret of its spiritual success is a largely-attended, fervent prayer meeting. It is still true that when Zion travails, she brings forth.

Extending a thought already expressed, namely, that a prayer meeting is what it purports to be—a meeting for prayer; it may be as well to explain what such a meeting *is not*. A prayer meeting is not a gathering for the exposition of Scripture. A Bible class has its important place and will be provided for by a pastor believing in a thorough and systematic unfolding of Scripture. Certainly, to invite prayer and intercession a suitable portion of the Word should be read at a prayer meeting. Neither is it to be a missionary meeting, at which missionaries tell the story of their work, or at which missionary letters and reports are given. This valuable type of meeting also has its place. Spirit-controlled prayer meetings exercise a mighty influence upon missionary work at home and abroad. Yet in the strict sense of the term, the prayer meeting is not a missionary meeting. The midweek service should not be a time to listen to a book review, a lecture, or an essay. The time allotted should be devoted to earnest, believing prayer, for a church living on her knees is invincible in a demonized world.

The Bible is explicit when it comes to those who should attend a prayer meeting. Those who are called to do service for the Master should be present.

> And when they were come in, they went up into an upper room, where abode both Peter, and James, and John, and Andrew, Philip, and Thomas, Bartholomew, and Matthew, James the son of Alphaeus, and Simon Zelotes, and Judas the brother of James. These all continued with one accord in prayer and supplication, with the women, and Mary the mother of Jesus, and with his brethren.
>
> (Acts 1:13–14)

This includes all office-bearers, choir and church members. Service without prayer is empty and hollow.

Godly women should attend the prayer meeting (see Acts 1:14), and women were present at the first gathering for prayer after Christ's ascension. Men should be ashamed of the fact that if it were not for the women, many prayer meetings would die. Proportionately, women do more for the church than do men.

All who were led to believe in Christ likewise were urged to attend a prayer meeting. (See Acts 1:14.) Aged saints were also found in the place of prayer.

> *And, behold, there was a man in Jerusalem, whose name was Simeon; and the same man was just and devout, waiting for the consolation of Israel: and the Holy Ghost was upon him. And it was revealed unto him by the Holy Ghost, that he should not see death, before he had seen the Lord's Christ. And he came by the Spirit into the temple: and when the parents brought in the child Jesus, to do for him after the custom of the law, then took he him up in his arms, and blessed God, and said, Lord, now lettest thou thy servant depart in peace, according to thy word: for mine eyes have seen thy salvation....And there was one Anna, a prophetess, the daughter of Phanuel, of the tribe of Aser: she was of a great age, and had lived with an husband seven years from her virginity; and she was a widow of about fourscore and four years, which departed not from the temple, but served God with fastings and prayers night and day.*   (Luke 2:25–30, 36–37)

Young believers attending all-night prayer meetings are not a modern invention. As recorded in Acts,

> *When he had considered the thing, he came to the house of Mary the mother of John, whose surname was Mark; where many were gathered together praying. And as Peter knocked at the door of the gate, a damsel came to hearken, named Rhoda.* (Acts 12:12–13)

Successful workers attended. "*Now Peter and John went up together into the temple at the hour of prayer, being the ninth hour*" (Acts 3:1). Turning to prayer prevented success from going to their heads. Troubled workers can also find relief at such a time. "*And now, Lord, behold their threatenings: and grant unto thy servants, that with all boldness they may speak thy word"* (Acts 4:29). What a balm the blessed hour of prayer can be to those who need strength and deliverance!

Young converts are among those who gather for prayer: *"And he leaping up stood, and walked, and entered with them into the temple, walking, and leaping, and praising God"* (Acts 3:8). It is to them that knowledge will come that prayer is a gift, increasing in value with its use. Older believers should be patient with the crude utterances of spiritual babes. Those newly liberated attended a prayer meeting in Acts. *"And being let go, they went to their own company, and reported all that the chief priests and elders had said unto them"* (Acts 4:23). *"Let go"* from the cares of business and of home. How refreshing it is to turn aside to pray with those who are like-minded.

Travelers from home went to a prayer meeting.

And on the sabbath we went out of the city by a river side, where prayer was wont to be made; and we sat down, and spake unto the women which resorted thither. And a certain woman named Lydia, a seller of purple, of the city of Thyatira, which worshipped God, heard us: whose heart the Lord opened, that she attended unto the things which were spoken of Paul. (Acts 16:13–14)

Can you not imagine Paul coming to a strange city and looking around for a gathering of praying saints? What do you do when away from home on business or on a vacation? In another city, is it your desire to find a place where prayer is apt to be made? Too many professing Christians, when away for a while from their home church, act as if they were not church members.

Because the human leadership of a prayer meeting is an important factor, it may prove profitable to consider one or two elements of success in this direction. The less of the human element, the better. A leader should not try to control a prayer meeting. Believing, as the early church did, in the presence and presidency of the Holy Spirit when they gathered together, we know that when He is in control, all things will be ordered correctly.

Long prayers should be discouraged and avoided. As Charles Spurgeon once said, "Length is a death-blow to earnestness, and brevity is an assistant to zeal." The leader should state definite matters for prayer, and prayer should be explicit. If, for instance, prayer is asked for a member in the hospital, prayer should be focused upon such a need, and not go out and embrace the world. Long prayers covering so much ground, not only monopolize time, but are weariness to the flesh. We are not heard for our much speaking.

All present, no matter how timid some are, should be encouraged to take part. In the early days of his Christian life, the present writer developed a desire to pray, by the system of chain-sentence prayers in the Christian Endeavour meeting. Hesitant, stumbling, ungrammatical prayers, prayers of those unaccustomed to the sound of their own voice in public, should never be criticized. God answers prayer, not according to our intelligence but His own. Women should be encouraged to pray as well as men. There is no proof in the New Testament that Christian women should be forbidden to exercise such a privilege. In fact Acts 1:14 says, *"These all continued with one accord in prayer and supplication, with the women, and Mary the mother of Jesus, and with his brethren."*

It makes for efficiency if the leader has special requests for prayer, for the same prevents aimlessness in praying. One has found it helpful to have a list of subjects on hand, and repeating one at a time, ask for two or three short prayers bearing on that subject mentioned.

Then it greatly adds to the spirit of the meeting if all present are urged to sit together as closely as possible. The closer the coal is, the brighter the blaze!

As for hymn singing, while one or two well-chosen devotional hymns, which are simply prayers set to music, incite one to pray, hymns and choruses should not eat up the time intended for definite prayer.

Punctuality, even for a prayer meeting, is not a crime. It should open and end as it was advertised, unless there are evidences of extraordinary expression, and the Spirit is moving and melting hearts. When

His leadership is relied upon, there will never be any doubt about pre-
scribed or prolonged seasons of prayer.

There were only two or three of us
Who came to the place of prayer;
Came in the teeth of a driving storm,
But for that we did not care.
Since after our hymns of praise had risen,
And our earnest prayers were said,
The Master Himself was present there,
And He gave us the Living Bread.
We knew His look on our leader's face,
So rapt, and glad, and free;
We felt His touch when our heads were bowed,
We heard His "Come to Me."
Nobody saw Him lift the latch,
And none unbarred the door,
But "peace" was His message to every heart,
And how could we seek for more?
Each of us felt the load of sin
From the weary shoulder fall;
Each of us dropped the load of care,
And the grief that was like a pall;
And over our spirit a blessed calm
Swept in from the jasper sea,
And strength was ours for toil and strife,
In the days that were thence to be.
It was only a handful gathered in
To the little place of prayer;
Outside were struggling and pain and sin,
But the Lord Himself was there.
He came to redeem the pledge He gave,
Wherever His loved ones be,
To stand Himself in the midst of them,
Though they count but two or three.

And forth we went in the bitter rain,
But our hearts had grown so warm
It seemed like a pelting of summer flowers,
And not the crush of the storm.
"'Twas a blessed hour of fellowship
At the Lord's right hand," we said,
As we thought of how Jesus Himself had come
To feed us with Living Bread.

13

EFFECTIVE TESTIMONY

Up until the baneful influences of Modernism were felt in Methodism, its churches had a weekly "experience meeting" when members would meet to testify to God's grace and goodness. Why has it almost vanished, not only from Methodism, but also from other branches of the Christian church? Can it be that the majority of members do not have an "experience" they can speak about? "Let the redeemed of the Lord say so." We have church societies galore. Why not institute a "Say-So Society" at which members should be urged to testify of a personal experience of Christ's saving and satisfying power? This lack of testimonies in a church is an evidence of profession without possession.

Outlining, as we are, practical and efficient methods of Christian work, let us give a little attention to the place of "testimony" in church life. There is no need to linger over the importance of a definite meeting, or part of a meeting, for testimonies. *Christian Science* recognizes the value of such a period for making known their particular tenets. The greater part of the time is devoted to witnessing to the supposed power of the cult, which is neither *Christian* nor *scientific*. Apart from Salvation

Army gatherings, and strongly evangelical, unaffiliated churches, the voices of the vast majority of church members are never publicly raised in testimony as to what Christ is or has done for them. This is a serious lack that ought to be remedied. The early church practiced the testimony meeting: *"How is it then, brethren? When ye come together, every one of you hath a psalm, hath a doctrine, hath a tongue, hath a revelation, hath an interpretation. Let all things be done unto edifying"* (1 Corinthians 14:26). And what stories those early saints had to tell! Their meetings must have been an inspiration!

Just where a testimony meeting could fit in with the highly organized church life of today is a difficult question. Where there is a will, however, there is a way, and any church stressing evangelism will see that provision is made for converts and more mature saints to give expression to their heart's gratitude for God's mercy. Of course, a leader guiding such a testimony or experience meeting will stress the necessity of having up-to-date testimonies. To hear the same old story time after time is not edifying. If a gathering of this nature is held once a week, or forms a part of another regular service, emphasis should be upon experiences overtaking the testifiers since they last met. Wisely guided, and conducted within limits, regular testimonies are a valuable adjunct to church work, and are attended with encouraging results.

To bear witness is biblical. "Witness" is one of the impressive words of the Bible, occurring over 100 times. The term itself simply means "telling out what we know," which is something young and old alike can do. Christ's last commission was taken up with a positive, definite testimony to the world of His reality. (See Acts 1:8; Luke 24:45.) As to the witness himself, his witness is only effective as he gives evidence of what Christ has been and is to him, personally. Secondhand evidence never results in the authority of experience. The testimony must be of what one has seen and heard. Further, personal worth must back up personal witness. Without character, confession is worthless. One's life must say "Amen!" to what the lips declare. As a believer seeks to give a reason of the hope within his heart, he will gladly testify of God's love, wisdom, grace, power, faithfulness, and sufficiency. He will witness to the practical power of faith in his own life and labors. (See Hebrews 11–12:2.)

Attention to the manner and spirit in witness will also aid its effectiveness. Any unpleasant or offensive manner robs a testimony of mutual influence. For example, when dealing with one's past, it is not advisable to drag out all the skeletons from the cupboard. As former deeds are under the blood of Christ, it is best to leave them there. Yet some seem to gloat over lurid descriptions of their past life of sin. Spurgeon said that he hated to "hear a man speak of his experience in sin as a Greenwich pensioner might of Trafalgar. The best thing to do with our past sin, if it be indeed forgiven, is to bury it." When testifying to God's saving grace, we should magnify such grace and relate the circumstances leading to conviction and conversion. Dealing with up-to-date experiences as Christians, we should relate God's care and providence. As we grow in grace, we always have something fresh to relate as to what Christ means to us and of what He accomplishes through us.

It should not be necessary to say that at all times we must be honest and truthful in testimony. We must stick rigidly to facts. Exaggeration should be shunned. Yet one has heard a "life story" presented in such a way as to create doubt as to the reliability of some of its facts. Gravity should also accompany a truthful testimony. Undue levity should be guarded against as should any cold, mechanical utterance. With heartstrings loosed, and in deepest reverence, our anointed lips should declare what God has done for our soul. And in and through our witness, the incentive must be the glory of God. Self-exaltation robs many a testimony of its power and effectiveness. Testifying, one should also bear in mind the edification of those who listen. Under the constraining power of love to Christ, one's speech must be fragrant with such a love. Only then can some lukewarm listener come to experience anew the glow of a lost devotion. Think of the many souls who have been saved, and backsliders restored, through the earnest, truthful, and loving testimony of those basking in the sunshine of God's forgiveness and favor!

Can it be that these lines are being read by those who once had a vibrant, victorious witness, but who allowed sin and the world to silence their lips? David, who had been so vocal with praise as he meditated upon the transcendent attributes of God, allowed a grievous sin to seal his lips. But forgiven, he prayed, "*O Lord, open thou my lips; and my mouth shall shew forth thy praise*" (Psalm 51:15). God, and those around you, miss your testimony. So, if in need of cleansing and restoration, why not seek it, and with live coal from off the altar touching your lips, go and tell.

> *Then said I, Woe is me! for I am undone; because I am a man of unclean lips, and I dwell in the midst of a people of unclean lips: for mine eyes have seen the King, the Lord of hosts. Then flew one of the seraphims unto me, having a live coal in his hand, which he had taken with the tongs from off the altar: and he laid it upon my mouth, and said, Lo, this hath touched thy lips; and thine iniquity is taken away, and thy sin purged. Also I heard the voice of the Lord, saying, Whom shall I send, and who will go for us? Then said I, Here am I; send me. And he said, Go, and tell this people, Hear ye indeed, but understand not; and see ye indeed, but perceive not.*
>
> (Isaiah 6:5–9)

Now just a word for Jesus,
Your dearest Friend so true;
Come cheer our hearts and tell us
What He has done for you.
Now just a word for Jesus,
A cross it cannot be
To say, I love my Savior
Who gave His life for me.

14

EFFECTIVE SINGING AND SONG LEADING

Since early Bible times, singing has been esteemed as an integral part of worship. Heathenism has no inspiring hymns, and Roman Catholicism does not employ a hymn book for public worship. It was Martin Luther, the converted monk, who set all Germany ablaze with religious enthusiasm as he sang his magnificent hymn, "Ein' Feste Burg" (A Mighty Fortress), in which his young friend, Melanchthon, and multitudes of believers, joined. The great evangelical revival under the Wesleys owed as much to the thrilling singing of the wonderful hymnist, Charles Wesley, as it did to the dynamic preaching of his famous brother, John. When the church came into being, historically, its only hymnbook was the book of Psalms, the Jewish praise book. Our Lord and His apostles used these inspired songs of praise which hymns of human composition will never be able to supersede. Pliny mentions that early Christians gathered and "sang hymns to Christ as God." The Reformation restored congregational singing which, under Romanism, had suffered an eclipse. Isaac

Watts is usually spoken of as the father of English hymnody, seeing he was about "the first both to articulate and to meet the need of Scriptural hymns which could be sung to usual psalm meters, voicing the praise of God's people in New Testament language."

We will never know how good gospel hymns have been used of God for the bringing of multitudes to Himself. Vast audiences have been moved and melted by the singing of dear departed saints, such as Ira D. Sankey, Charles M. Alexander, and George Beverly Shea. What soul-saving stories could be told of the influence of hymns, like "Jesus, Lover of My Soul"; "Rock of Ages"; "There Is a Fountain Filled with Blood"; "Just as I Am"; "Softly and Tenderly Jesus is Calling." General congregational singing in church or evangelistic services has resulted in the transformation of many souls.

In the Old Testament we have the Song of Redemption: "*And Miriam the prophetess, the sister of Aaron, took a timbrel in her hand; and all the women went out after her with timbrels and with dances. And Miriam answered them, Sing ye to the LORD, for he hath triumphed gloriously; the horse and his rider hath he thrown into the sea*" (Exodus 15:20–21). For other examples of singing, look at:

> *And the king made of the almug trees pillars for the house of the Lord, and for the king's house, harps also and psalteries for singers: there came no such almug trees, nor were seen unto this day.*
>
> (1 Kings 10:12)

> *And David spake to the chief of the Levites to appoint their brethren to be the singers with instruments of musick, psalteries and harps and cymbals, sounding, by lifting up the voice with joy....So the singers, Heman, Asaph, and Ethan, were appointed to sound with cymbals of brass....And David was clothed with a robe of fine linen, and all the Levites that bare the ark, and the singers, and Chenaniah the master of the song with the singers: David also had upon him an ephod of linen.*
>
> (1 Chronicles 15:16, 19, 27)

It came even to pass, as the trumpeters and singers were as one, to make one sound to be heard in praising and thanking the LORD; and when they lifted up their voice with the trumpets and cymbals and instruments of musick, and praised the LORD, saying, For he is good; for his mercy endureth for ever: that then the house was filled with a cloud, even the house of the Lord.

(2 Chronicles 5:13)

*The singers: the children of Asaph, an hundred twenty and eight....
So the priests, and the Levites, and some of the people, and the singers, and the porters, and the Nethinims, dwelt in their cities, and all Israel in their cities.*   (Ezra 2:41, 70)

In Nehemiah, singers and singing are mentioned some seventeen times. In the New Testament, singing is prominent. Angels and men are found singing:

And suddenly there was with the angel a multitude of the heavenly host praising God, and saying, Glory to God in the highest, and on earth peace, good will toward men....And the shepherds returned, glorifying and praising God for all the things that they had heard and seen, as it was told unto them.   (Luke 2:13–14, 20)

Saying, Blessed be the King that cometh in the name of the Lord: peace in heaven, and glory in the highest.   (Luke 19:38)

And at midnight Paul and Silas prayed, and sang praises unto God: and the prisoners heard them.   (Acts 16:25)

I will pray with the spirit, and I will pray with the understanding also: I will sing with the spirit, and I will sing with the understanding also....How is it then, brethren? when ye come together, every one of you hath a psalm, hath a doctrine, hath a tongue, hath a revelation, hath an interpretation. Let all things be done unto edifying.   (1 Corinthians 14:15, 26)

Speaking to yourselves in psalms and hymns and spiritual songs,
singing and making melody in your heart to the Lord.

(Ephesians 5:19)

Let the word of Christ dwell in you richly in all wisdom; teaching
and admonishing one another in psalms and hymns and spiritual
songs, singing with grace in your hearts to the Lord.

(Colossians 3:16)

Is any among you afflicted? Let him pray. Is any merry? Let him
sing psalms.   (James 5:13)

The apostolic, triple division of Ephesians 5:19 is worthy of note:

1. There are *"psalms,"* doubtless an Old Testament psalm
    accompanied by a musical instrument, the like of which is
    now banned by some religious groups.

2. By are *"hymns,"* we understand a song of praise to God. The
    Greek word translated as *hymn* is *humnos*, signifying a musi-
    cal ode in honor of a god or a hero. In discussing any basic
    difference between a "psalm" or a "hymn," Bernard Martin
    says that "David's psalms are 'musical odes' in honor of God.
    Christian hymns are 'musical odes' in honor of God, the Son,
    and the Holy Spirit. Thus it is seen that there is not really a
    basic difference between psalms and hymns, and these terms
    are, in fact, sometimes used interchangeably. For example,
    the Lord and His disciples, in singing psalms, are stated to
    have sung 'a hymn'. Undoubtedly the two words are used
    by Paul to distinguish between the inspired songs already
    in use, and the Spirit-indited songs of believers in the new
    dispensation."

3. Spiritual songs are those on a spiritual theme such as can
    be found in Ephesians 5:19. Rigid distinctions, however,
    cannot be pressed, seeing that a tribute of praise can be a
    psalm, hymn, or spiritual song.

Luke gives us five songs, all of which are related to Christ's Advent:

1. The Song of the Annunciation (Luke 1:28, 35): "Ave Maria"

2. The Song of the Virgin (Luke 1:46–55): "The Magnificat"

3. The Song of Zacharias (Luke 1:68–79): "Benedictus"

4. The Song of the Angels (Luke 2:14): "Gloria in Excelsis"

5. The Song of Simeon (Luke 2:29–32): "Nunc Dimittis"

All who preach the Word realize the influence and importance of gospel singing. "The Song message is a preparation for the spoken message." The effectiveness of the ministry of song cannot be overstated. God's Spirit mightily uses hymns, sung with artless assurance and joy. Gospel songs, however, are only effective, whether sung as solos or by a congregation, as certain facts are observed:

First of all, let us think of the singers themselves: song leaders, soloists, the choir, the congregation. It should not be necessary to state that it is imperative for a song leader to be converted and consecrated if he is to lead the praise of others. What mockery it is for him to try and lead an audience in singing "Take my life and let it be consecrated, Lord, to Thee," if he himself is unsaved! If truly saved, he should guard against ostentation. Parade of ability is obnoxious. Jewelry, too, should be used sparingly. It can distract attention when it jangles or flashes. He must also remember that while his ministry is a valuable adjunct to the preacher's work, he must not be guilty of monopolizing the preacher's time. Too often, even well-meaning song-leaders murder a meeting by too much singing. People are exhausted by the time the preacher gets to them.

As to all who form a choir, the same principle holds good. All choir members must be those who know the Lord, otherwise they are Sunday liars, singing of God's grace and sanctifying power, yet having hearts destitute of salvation. Spurgeon remarked that too often "the choir is the war department of a church." Another has remarked that "the choir of a church is always a storm centre from which proceeds a considerable amount of lightning, even if this should not be accompanied by volleys of thunder." Choir members should never forget that inattention while the preacher is presenting his message is a crime. To chatter, write notes, fidget, read, or act bored as they sit the sermon out creates a bad impression. They must remember that all eyes are upon them, as well as upon the preacher. Of course, all that we are saying goes also for organist or instrumentalist. Those who play, like those who sing, must be men and women of spirituality of heart and of undoubted Christian character.

Those who take solo parts, or who are known as soloists, must not only be efficient as far as musical accomplishment is concerned, but they must sing without affectation. Self must be hid. Solos must be rendered feelingly, pleadingly, and with full reliance upon the Spirit's power to make the song an avenue of blessing.

As to the choice of suitable hymns, much might be written. The old Moody and Sankey hymnbooks contain hundreds of most scriptural and appealing hymns. What unforgettable tunes they have! True, some of them may be defective, lyrically, but God has mightily used them for the salvation of souls.

When it comes to the close of a message or a meeting, great care must be exercised in the selection of an invitation hymn. A suitable appeal clinches the earnest plea of the preacher. For those on the point of decision use "I am coming to the cross," or "Thou, O Christ, art all I want." Those who need to be confirmed in assurance are helped by "Hallelujah, 'tis done, I believe on the Son." Those who hesitate are often led to decision by the use of "Just as I am"—perhaps the most used invitation hymn we have. "Almost persuaded" and "Pass me not, O Gentle Saviour" have also stood the test of years as extra pleaders for the soul's surrender to the claims of Christ.

Now and again it is effective to tell the story of a hymn—how it came to be written and incidents associated with the use of it around the world.

15

EFFECTIVE PERSONAL EVANGELISM

From her inception, the church's establishment and extension have depended upon evangelism. With her it is a matter of evangelize or fossilize. Personal evangelism should be the main purpose and the persistent aim of a Christian worker. Asking oneself the question, "How can I best lay out my life for God in my generation?" What other answer can be given than that of the dedication of one's time and talents for the supreme task of winning souls to Christ.

It will be borne in mind that in this section we are not dealing with mass or professional evangelism, but with the personal evangelism Andrew practiced when he brought his brother to Jesus. *"One of the two which heard John speak, and followed him, was Andrew, Simon Peter's brother. He first findeth his own brother Simon, and saith unto him, we have found the Messias, which is, being interpreted, the Christ"* (John 1:40–41). We have become too dependent upon united efforts, combined revivals, with their usual retinue of advance men, advertising agents, magnetic preachers, and parties of choristers and workers. Yet in spite of all such efforts, and the expenditure of large sums of money, the great mass of unsaved are not even touched. The secret of reaching the unchurched multitudes is personal evangelism on the part of those within the Church. We sadly need in every church a strong and vigorous "Society of Andrews," pledged to bring relatives, friends, neighbors, business associates, to Christ. And it is the solemn responsibility of pastors to urge upon their people the necessity of speaking a good word for Jesus Christ wherever they may live or labor. *"A man hath joy by the answer of his mouth: and a word spoken in due season, how good is it!"* (Proverbs 15:23). *"The Lord God hath given me the tongue of the learned, that I should know how to speak a word in season to him that is weary: he wakeneth morning by morning, he wakeneth mine ear to hear as the learned"* (Isaiah 50:4).

This need of personal evangelism is evident. In Britain not more than 10 percent of the population darkens a church door. In America, while church membership is at an all-time high, there are yet millions who have no interest whatsoever in God or His house. Every city and town forms a great field for personal workers watching for souls. Spurgeon said, "Hand-gathered fruit is best and keeps best."

Opportunities for personal evangelism are as varied as they are rare. At work, on the street, traveling by bus or train or plane, in stores, over the fence, wherever souls are to be found, there is also an opportunity for this type of service. A man at the Northfield Conference in D. L. Moody's time was asked by a reporter if he could direct him to a certain gentleman attending. "I am very sorry," the Christian said, "that I cannot direct you; had you asked me the way to heaven, I could have told you that. Do you know the way to heaven?" he continued.

"No," said the reporter, "I cannot say that I do."

"Well, it is just this," said the wide-awake worker and then went on to explain the way of salvation, which resulted in the reporter's conversion.

The daily round of life offers many opportunities of soul-winning. Jesus believed in this wayside ministry as the conversation at the well so clearly proves (see John 4), in the way He met an opportunity and used it to the full. Witnessing in this fashion, it is surprising how many one meets whose hearts are hungry for spiritual things. Some of them were longing for someone to speak to them about the things that matter most in life. Over ten years ago, in England, the archbishops of Canterbury and York set up a commission to survey the whole problem of evangelism. The findings of this commission are contained in the report, *Towards the Conversion of England*, published in 1945. Here is a telling phrase from the report—"We are convinced that England will never be converted until the laity use the opportunities for evangelism daily afforded by their various professions, crafts, and occupations."

Such an observation is also true of any other country. Factories, shops, stores, banks, and all aspects of professional and industrial life offer avenues of witness. The secular work by which the vast majority must live should be dedicated to Christ as the medium of evangelism.

There is no need to stress the importance of winning souls for Christ. One has only to consider the place such a mission has in the mind of God, and in the life, labors, and teachings of Christ, to realize that the whole plan of redemption was conceived in order to accomplish the rescue of the lost. We do the most for the world when we seek to make disciples of those we contact in the little piece of the world we represent.

Effectiveness in such God-honoring work depends upon a few factors. In the first place, we must have a love and a passion for the lost. The spirit and sacrifice of David Brainerd must be ours. "I cared not where or how I lived, or what hardships I went through, so that I could but gain souls for Christ." Romans 9:1–3 agrees: *"I say the truth in Christ, I lie not, my conscience also bearing me witness in the Holy Ghost, That I have great heaviness and continual sorrow in my heart. For I could wish that myself were accursed from Christ for my brethren, my kinsmen according to the flesh."* Of this passage, Dr. Campbell Morgan says that it is the utterance of "the daring of a great soul who longs for others." Such a passion became ours as we meditated upon what God has accomplished in order that souls might be saved—upon a deep and heartfelt conviction of the soul's worth—upon the terrible eternity awaiting all who die out of Christ.

> Oh, for a passionate passion for souls!
> Oh, for a pity that yearns!
> Oh, for a love that loves unto death,
> Oh, for a fire that burns!
> Oh, for a prayer power that prevails,
> That pours itself out for the lost;
> Victorious prayer in the Conqueror's name,
> Oh, for a Pentecost!

In the next place, the worker eager to win others, either at his daily task or during his off hours, will pray much about a fitting contact. If he concentrates upon a lost friend, interceding for him that in some way the opportunity may come his way to speak to his friend about Christ, He will bring about the contact! And when the two meet, it will be found that the Lord prepared the soil for the seed.

Once contact has been made, then tact is necessary in the presentation of the gospel. At times, over-anxiousness or an injudicious approach repels the soul we seek to win. There may be times when a bold, instant approach is effective, but usually it is best to be tactful as Paul was when he adapted himself to the needs of those he sought to win. (See 1 Corinthians 9:20.) Tact is described as "a quick or instinctive appreciation of what is fit, proper, or right; fine or ready mental discernment, shown in saying or doing the proper thing, or especially in avoiding what would offend or disturb; skill or faculty in dealing with men or emergencies." Is this not the very faculty the soul-winner needs?

Our English word *tact* comes from the Latin word meaning "to touch." Tact is having just the right touch.

Some people have it. When little Johnny bumps himself, and is more frightened than hurt, "Mommy kisses it all better." She has tact.

The born nurse can arrange the pillows for a fevered patient so that they are just right. A wife who wants some household chore done, suggests that she could wipe the dishes herself tonight, if friend husband would be so kind as to do—the task in mind. She has tact. A commercial traveler presents a window display to a merchant to increase sales of some common article. He has tact.

Some people lack it. A personal worker who sincerely desires to lead souls to Christ accosts a rather shy young man across the dinner table, in the presence of the family. "Tom, are you saved?" he may ask, and thus cause such embarrassment that he does not "touch" that soul. Another engages a man in conversation about every day affairs; and when the man speaks appreciatively of some questionable amusement, the would-be evangelist denounces trivialities in a way that makes the Christian life seem merely a system of taboos. Still another earnest Christian meets at his church a visitor who has attended some other place of worship that, to be frank, does not preach the gospel, and proceeds to express his own loyalty to Christian truth in terms that are highly offensive. The visitor may be polite enough to listen, but probably he will not again expose himself to such abuse.

Boldness? Yes, Lord, give us holy boldness, but with it give us tact. An elderly evangelist was leading devotional exercises in a Baptist convention. We do not usually laugh at prayers, but this time the expression was too much for our religious composure. Yet it is a prayer we all might utter:

"Lord, give us tact—not tacks, Lord, but tact." Too many of us spread *tacks*, but they cause those we seek to win to wince!

God has promised us wisdom for the all-important task of winning souls, and the tactful worker will pray, plan, and watch.

Sometimes it is well to refrain for a time from speaking about spiritual things, because the one to whom we are speaking is expecting to be dealt with and is prejudiced. D. L. Moody was an expert at soul-winning, and sometimes, knowing the one he sought to win had steeled himself against personal dealing, would not speak upon these vital matters for a time. Upon one occasion, without mentioning religion, Moody played tennis all the afternoon with a young man who was expecting to be buttonholed straightaway. It was after he had won the young man to himself that he won him to Christ.

The tactful worker will not intrude when the person is overwhelmed with business, nor rebuke a man when he is angry. By waiting for a time of leisure, it will be found that the busy man has an open mind, and the angry man will have cooled down, and probably will have seen his folly before you speak. If the advance made about spiritual things is met with a rebuff, it is well to close the conversation with a kind remark and show there is no ill-feeling, speaking about some general subject to terminate the encounter.

In the old coaching days, Robert Murray McCheyne was traveling from Perth to Aberdeen, and after general conversation with a lady passenger in the coach, put a pointed question concerning her spiritual condition. She replied indignantly, "Sir, I am a bishop's daughter." Whereupon McCheyne courteously said, "Madam, I could have wished you were the daughter of a King." A few days later he received a letter from the lady, in which she said she could now sign herself as "a King's daughter."

If all qualifications are striven for, then success can be expected, as we speak to the lost in the way. While it is true that it is the soul-winner's responsibility to labor faithfully and leave results with God, it would be a strange thing if He prompted us to sow seed and forbade us to look for harvest, or to fish for souls and expect no catch. Success is promised to those who seek to "rescue the perishing":

> *He that goeth forth and weepeth, bearing precious seed, shall doubtless come again with rejoicing, bringing his sheaves with him.*
>
> (Psalm 126:6)

> *And they that be wise shall shine as the brightness of the firmament; and they that turn many to righteousness as the stars for ever and ever.*
>
> (Daniel 12:3)

Brethren, if any of you do err from the truth, and one convert him;
Let him know, that he which converteth the sinner from the error of
his way shall save a soul from death, and shall hide a multitude of
sins.   (James 5:19–20)

And again, I will put my trust in him. And again, behold I and the
children which God hath given me.   (Hebrews 2:13)

A revival of personal evangelism, such as we have indicated, would bring about a mighty spiritual upheaval in the land. We have become too dependent upon planned revivals and evangelistic campaigns, professional evangelists and revivalists, and upon all the paraphernalia of crowd-gathering techniques. It is high time to return to the apostolic method of winning souls, one by one. If every church member would win a soul for Christ in two weeks, what a marvelous impact the ultimate result would have upon the church and community!

16

EFFECTIVE TRACT DISTRIBUTION

Eternity alone will reveal what leaflet evangelism has meant to the cause of Christ. Millions upon millions of silent messengers have scattered the message of salvation far and wide. Gospel tracts are the cheapest and most highly effective way of reaching the lost. The files of a renowned Tract Society like that of the *American Tract Society*, operating for over 125 years, are filled with testimonials of God's working through what might seem to many to be "an insignificant tract." The popular tract "Four Things God Wants You to Know" prevented a murder in Norfolk, Virginia. Here is the story of a woman in the mountains who picked up a small tract of Dr. Bob Jones Sr., out of a mud hole, carried it home, dried and cleansed it, read it, and found the Lord. In turn she led her husband and family to Christ.

Tract distribution affords an avenue of service for the vast army of voluntary workers in churches over the land. In fact, it will be found that the bulk of tracts are purchased by lay workers and scattered by them in all kinds of ways. There is no simpler method with which those who are newly saved can engage in Christian service. Christian businessmen; employees in shops, offices, and factories; travelers in cars, trains, and planes, employ the tract to enter into conversation with others. In hotels, at airports, railway and bus stations, these silent messengers can be found. The old evangelistic practice of tract distribution, more prominent than ever, has been copied, with great effect, by the Romanists, Christian Scientists, and other false cults. The value of the tract has been summarized thus:

> Tracts can go everywhere. Tracts know no fear. Tracts never tire. Tracts can be multiplied without end by the press. Tracts can travel at little expense. They run up and down like the angels of God, blessing all, giving to all, asking no gift in return. They can talk to one as well as to a multitude, and to a multitude as well as one. They require no public room to tell their story in. They can tell it in the kitchen or the shop, the parlor or the closet, in the railway coach or on the bus, on the broad highway or in the footpath through the foothills. They take no note of scoffs or jeers or taunts. No one can betray them into hasty or random expressions. Though they will not always answer questions, they will tell their stories twice or thrice or four times if you wish them to. And they can be made to speak on every subject, and on every subject they may be made to speak wisely and well. They can, in short, be made the vehicles of truth, the teachers of all classes, and the benefactor of all saints.

The purpose and power of tract distribution inspires multitudes of lay workers to invest some of their money in suitable tracts and then carry them around and wisely scatter them. Thus bread is cast upon the waters and found after many days: *"Cast thy bread upon the waters: for thou shalt find it after many days"* (Ecclesiastes 11:1). It was a tract handed to saintly Richard Baxter of Kidderminster that resulted in his salvation. In turn, Baxter wrote "Saints' Everlasting Rest" which led Philip Doddridge to pen, "Rise and Progress of Religion in the Soul," through which William Wilberforce was converted. Wilberforce wrote "Practical Christianity," which fell into the hands of Thomas Chalmers, the mighty Scottish preacher who became Founder of the Free Church of Scotland. It was a tract that first moved John Bunyan to think of spiritual things. Hudson Taylor, famous missionary to China and Founder of the China Inland Mission, was brought to Christ when a boy, through a tract handed to him. D. L. Moody recognized the power of the tract. During the World's Fair in Chicago he distributed over half a million tracts. In turn he founded the Bible Colportage Society which printed and circulated millions of tracts and gospel booklets, and is now The Moody Press. Spurgeon was another who used leaflet evangelism to great effect. Countless thousands have been blessed through his tracts. Loyal, devoted volunteer Christian workers will find heaven full of joyful surprises as they meet many on the streets of gold won to the Savior along the way through tracts they prayerfully distributed.

The mission of tracts must never be underestimated. What effective messengers of Christ they are! Think of the influence they exert. Tracts are widely used in the salvation of souls, succeeding when a sermon fails to reach the heart.

Tracts counteract erroneous teaching and are effective in combating the evil influence of unwholesome literature.

Tracts encourage the doubting and depressed, comfort the sorrowing. Countless thousands have been raised to higher heights through the printed message. A tract like "Steps to and in the Blessed Life," by A. T. Pierson, placed in letters, has brought a deeper spiritual life to souls everywhere.

If gospel tracts are to be effective when distributed, certain principles must be kept in mind if the worker is out to obtain the best results. All tract users want their ministry to be fruitful, as they send silent messengers on their way. Here, then, are necessary methods to observe:

1. *Distribute tracts prayerfully.* Let no tract be given away that is not first of all steeped in prayer that it might reach a soul. The

distributor needs to pray that he or she might be guided to the right person and then present the right tract.

2. *Distribute tracts appropriately.* A tract should fit the need of the person approached. One has heard of a worker giving a tract stressing the evils of dancing to a man with a wooden leg. Another gave a tract of mixed marriage to an elderly bachelor.

3. *Distribute tracts courteously.* Never thrust them into the hands of a person as if you were doing something distasteful. Offer them with a smile, as a salesman would close a deal in the friendliest manner. Tracts are seldom refused when offered graciously and with a genuinely friendly smile.

4. *Distribute tracts patiently.* Never resent a rebuff. Never force a tract upon a passerby. Indiscriminate tract distribution is a waste of time and money. A sidewalk littered with rejected tracts cheapens the cause of leaflet evangelism.

5. *Distribute attractive tracts.* A tract should attract. In these days of modern, illustrative printing, and expert proofreading, the old dry-looking and badly-written tracts are out of place. Arrestive, well-written, pictorial tracts can be secured from renowned printers like the American Tract Society, New York; the Berean Gospel Distributors, Indianapolis, Indiana; the Stirling Tract Enterprise, Stirling, Scotland; or the Victory Tract Club, Croydon, England.

As to ways and methods of distributing tracts, anyone with a little ingenuity can always think up avenues of using them. They can be used in personal letters, in greeting cards, in books we borrow, in bills we pay. Judiciously we can employ tracts when visiting prisons, hospitals, and other institutions. They can be used on trains and buses, in house-to-house visitation, and placed in out-of-the-way places.

Tracts may be dropped into a mailbox or in at an open window. They may be left in a house, a shop, the waiting room of the railway station, a taxi-cab, between the leaves of books—anywhere, in fact, where they are likely to be found. The finder might sometimes be impressed and induced to read by the very singularity of the place where the tract was found. An invalid mother, who was most solicitous for the conversion of her sons, inserted two or three tracts into their pockets that they might come upon them unaware. Love had found a way, and I have no doubt but that she will rejoice in the conversion of her boys. "Blessed are they who sow beside all waters." (See Isaiah 32:20.)

Discussing varied hindrances to effective tract distribution, Joseph W. Kemp says that we may look for opposition to such a laudable way of witnessing for Christ in these directions:

1. By ridicule. Sometimes there will be the shake of the head or the scornful look; sometimes even personal abuse, but these things, which are often the expression of deep conviction, will do the tract distributor no harm, but oftentimes a world of good.

2. Direct antagonism will also be met. One friend used to tell that forty years ago he narrowly escaped a martyr's crown in a railway journey to Portsmouth. "I was quietly handing out some Gospel tracts in one of the large, old-fashioned, low-partitioned third-class carriages, when with a great rage a man rose and held a revolver to my head, threatening to shoot me there and then unless I desisted. The passengers all seemed greatly alarmed and a scene occurred, amid which, coward as I too often am, I felt quite undisturbed, for soldiers of the King must sometimes be under fire."

3. Resentment will sometimes be faced. The saintly Murray McCheyne of Dundee made tract-distribution part of his daily life. One day he gave a tract to a fashionable lady who said to him, "Surely you do not know who I am." McCheyne replied: "He hath appointed a day in which He will judge the world, and unless you trust Him, you will stand no chance on that day, no matter who you are." We should pray for such as we meet them in our work.

4. Legal restrictions may obtain in certain cities, and tract distribution may be forbidden. Care should be exercised by Christian workers to find out the attitude of local authorities before undertaking the work.

The careful worker, who seeks to distribute clean-looking as well as constructive tracts during his spare time, will not take advantage of time that is not his own, that is, time when he is paid by an employer to pursue a given occupation. One recalls a friend more zealous than judicious, who had a good position in a hat shop for men. He always carried tracts in his pocket, and after selling a man a hat, when he came to wrap it up, would always slip a tract in. Finally, he lost his position over his lack of wisdom. What we do in our own time is our responsibility, but what we do when employed at a given wage to accomplish a given task is another matter, even in tract distribution, and has heed of wisdom. Tract distribution is such a God-honoring and soul-transforming work; let us not spoil it by ineffective, unwise methods.

17

EFFECTIVE OPEN-AIR WITNESS

In these days of modern transportation when, because of the hazard of automobile traffic, it is nearly impossible to hold an open-air meeting in a market place or at a street corner, it would seem as if this aspect of effective witness is redundant. Open-air work, however, has not completely died out. Bands of workers like those belonging to the Salvation Army, the Gideons, the Christian Business Men's Connection, rescue missions, and fundamental churches still find ways of going out into the highways to preach the gospel. It is for these open-air witnesses, who are almost one hundred per cent voluntary, that we include this aspect of service in our meditation. It is because the one penning these lines owes so much to open-air meetings in the earlier years of his Christian life that he approaches such a form of service with enthusiasm.

It is to be doubted whether there is any avenue of service that has had a more glorious history or accomplished as much for the souls of men than that of open-air witness. The long and honorable roll of Old Testament prophets testifies to the effectiveness of outdoor ministry. John, the Lord's forerunner, could gather a congregation in the desert place. Jesus Himself was an active open-air worker. His musical voice was often heard on the mountainside, in the plains, at the seaside, and on the sea. What an open-air meeting that must have been on the Day of Pentecost, as Peter preached! *"But Peter, standing up with the eleven, lifted up his voice, and said unto them, Ye men of Judaea, and all ye that dwell at Jerusalem, be this known unto you, and hearken to my words….Therefore they that were scattered abroad went every where preaching the word"* (Acts 2:14; 8:4)! The early fathers of the church did their share of open-air preaching under the canopy of the heavens. All down the church age, men and women with a burden for the lost have carried the message of salvation out under "the blue ethereal dome." Bishop Ryle says, of the old-time Methodists, that they preached everywhere, "In the field, or by the roadside; on the village green or in the market place, in lanes, or in alleys." John Wesley himself insisted that open-air preaching was one of the secrets of the growth of Methodism. As the fiery evangelist of the highways and byways of England, he wrote, "What a victory Satan would gain if he could put an end to field-preaching!" And he continued, "But I trust he never will—at least, not till my head is laid low." A precise and scholarly man, Wesley yet became the most effective open-air preacher the church has ever had.

Because of the dearth of church attendance, the need for this type of work is greater than ever. The masses will not come to the church, so the church must go to the masses. Seraphic George Whitefield, whose marvelous voice could reach thousands in the open air, *without the aid of a loud speaker system,* remarked that "there is no pulpit like a mound, no sounding board like heaven." Yet in our churches we are satisfied to struggle along with a few members, often content to fatten on one another's members, while outside there are countless multitudes waiting to be won. Professor William Clow may be right in his contention that "Open-air preaching is *the only way left to us* of gaining access to millions of hearts. It must be attempted and if attempted in the right way, it will be found amazingly successful." When engaged in, it should not be treated as a *mere extra* to church work, but as an essential contribution to the church's growth.

Because of present-day traffic problems creating a difficulty in conducting open-air meetings in a public thoroughfare, many churches might solve the problem by conducting a thirty-minute service on the church steps, around which people could gather with not much pedestrian obstruction. If held before an indoor service, such an outdoor service would fulfill a two-fold purpose, namely, give passersby the gospel message and at the same time invite people into the regular service. It was following a pre-indoor service like this that Billy Sunday, who became America's great evangelist, was converted. Invited into the Pacific Garden Mission by earnest open-air workers, Sunday reached his hour of decision.

What a profound impression churches would create if only they would go out to the unchurched masses! They would find that fresh air is not only good for the soil, but the *soul* as well. Samuel Chadwick of Cliff College, England, once said that "some churches might be saved if they were shut up for a few weeks, and all the services held in the fields or streets. The effect upon preachers would be better than a college course. It would develop their chests and save doctor's bills. It would loose them and let them go; and some of them have not been let go for years. Indoor religion gets anemic. Dim religious light and doleful windows develop all sorts of nervous disorders. A wholesale series of church-fires would be a godsend to the Christianity of the country, if it drove the churches to unconsecrated buildings and open spaces." These descriptive lines, by C. Field, of an English street preacher, are most expressive:

> "No crowd encircled him about;
> He stood despised with two or three,
> But like a spring in summer drought,
> The word he uttered quickened me.
> Around us Oxford, dome and tower,
> Majestic, breathed her charm august;
> But which of all her spells had power,

To raise the wretched from the dust?
What Oxford could not, Jesus did,
Bared to my eyes the depths of grace,
And all the unguessed treasures hid,
Beneath the dust of commonplace.
Since then I tread the pilgrim's way,
Still plodding on through sun and rain,
But like a star shines out that day,
That day which saw me born again.

As to our equipment for the task before us, while it demands the best we can bring to it, yet seeing that the majority forming a band of open-air workers are devoted Christians serving God in such a way in their own time, preparation that a candidate for the ministry might make is denied them. Certainly students in seminaries and Bible institutes should be compelled to undergo a course in open-air preaching, so that they could function as effective and efficient leaders. While great intellectual requirements are not absolutely essential, yet no gift or attainment is too valuable an asset to bring to this work. The day is past when we think that anything will do for the open air, where the main purpose is to reach non-churchgoers for Christ. Many students training for the work of the Lord have found their legs in street and shop meetings. They were put on their mettle, developed lungs and chest, learned how to preach without notes, and discovered the value of looking people in the eye and approaching them directly with the gospel.

For those who are denied necessary training, however, there are several ways by which they can equip themselves to become effective open-air witnesses. First of all, they must steep their hearts and minds in prayer and in the Scriptures. This will enable them, like Ezra, the ancient open-air preacher, to give the divine sense of the Word as, in their simple way, they proclaim it. *"So they read in the book in the law of God distinctly, and gave the sense, and caused them to understand the reading"* (Nehemiah 8:8). Then they must settle at the very outset of their witness that it is not their province to discuss politics or current events. Their business is to preach the saving truth of the gospel. They must keep within the range where the deepest needs of men cannot be lost sight of. In the wilderness, John caused "the generation of vipers to flee from the wrath to come" as he preached on sin, repentance, salvation, and judgment. The worker must guard against being dragged into controversy or into a tirade against those of another religion. It will repay him a thousand-fold to keep near the four R's: ruin, redemption, regeneration, and reception. Archibald C. Brown, close friend of C. H. Spurgeon, addressing open-air preachers, urged them to preach the gospel always. Said he:

1. The gospel is a *fact*: therefore tell it *simply*.

2. It is a *joyful* fact: therefore tell it *cheerily*.

3. It is an *entrusted* fact: therefore tell it *faithfully*.

4. It is a *fact of infinite moment*: therefore tell it *earnestly*.

5. It is a *fact of infinite love*: therefore tell it *pathetically*.

6. It is a *fact difficult of comprehension* to many: therefore tell it with *illustrations*.

7. It is a *fact about a Person*: therefore *preach Christ*.

Although the message may be short and simple, it should be well prepared and given persuasively. The worker will find that as he faces a moving crowd he will need resourcefulness as well as resources. No matter how well regulated the meeting, interruptions will occur, and to meet them, the open-air worker must be on the alert. An objector outside the ring may raise his voice disagreeing with the speaker, but all controversy and argument must be avoided. He must remain courteous, good-tempered, and cheerful, sticking to his message. The chief causes of interruption are drunks, who will want to argue, or call for a hymn, or may interfere with workers. Patience, tact, and firmness will be required to deal with the relatives of "John Barleycorn." Usually a drunken person can be led away gently by one of the workers and dealt with away from the crowd. If there are restrictions against holding outside meetings, the same should be respected. Some with a martyr-complex have disobeyed police regulations and have had to go to prison.

Authorities are usually sympathetic toward all gospel effort, where such can be engaged in without any complaint or traffic block.

One or two further suggestions as to the conduct of an effective meeting are in order. As singing plays an important part in this important phase of Christian service, let us think of it for a moment. Hymns, for example, should be chosen beforehand and should be of a popular sort. The old hymns, which many of the godless in the crowd may have heard in childhood days while attending Sunday school, will stir memories. If at all possible, there should be musical accompaniment and all hymns should be well and clearly sung. Good use should be made of efficient soloists, who usually gather a crowd in short time. The leader, announcing a hymn, should be ready to give a brief account of its composition, or some telling story associated with it. There should be plenty of hymn sheets on hand to lend to those surrounding the workers, who are sympathetic and would like to join in the singing. Variety should be aimed at. The leader will see to it that as many as possible take part in the meeting. One or two will render special musical numbers. There should be solos, duets, quartettes. Several short testimonies are impressive. Repetition of Scripture verses around the ring of workers also gets the gospel across. Then there will be a few instrumental items to add interest to the meeting. Those who give a short message should cultivate a complete command of the voice. It is injurious to speak or sing *against* a wind. There is no need to scream, roar, or shout. John Wesley's advice to open-air preachers should be borne in mind: "Scream no more at the peril of your soul. God warns you by me, whom He has set over you. Speak as earnestly as you can, but do not scream. Speak with all your heart, but with moderate voice. It was said of our Lord, 'He shall not cry.' The word means properly, 'He shall not scream.' Herein be a follower of me as I am of Christ. I often speak loud, even vehemently, but I never scream: I never strain myself: I dare not. I know it would be a sin against God and my own soul." Spurgeon has similar advice in his "Lectures to Students." In street preaching, he says, "A quiet, penetrating, conversational style would seem to be the most telling."

A final word is necessary as to follow-up work after the meeting has ended. Personal workers will linger to deal with any who seem to be impressed by what they heard. If the whole meeting was immersed in prayer, there are bound to be results glorifying to God.

18

EFFECTIVE VISITATION

Among other outside activities of loyal workers who seek to serve Christ in their spare time is that of visitation, whether it be house-to-house, prison, hospital, or other forms of visitation. Such a phase of Christian work, when properly undertaken, is productive of great results. Pastors know that systematic visitation of the right quality is an indispensable requisite of a fruitful ministry. They are not long in discovering that nearness to the lives of people and knowledge of their needs help shape his messages. Paul, speaking of his own settled ministry in Ephesus, tells us that he went from *house to house*, warning those who gathered of eternal verities. We are not dealing, however, with pastoral visitation, but with that devoted band of lay workers who either assist the pastor or undertake it on their own.

Let us take *house-to-house visitation* first of all. Prospects for church membership, unconverted people but deeply interested in spiritual things, sick and shut-in and afflicted men and women, the dying, the bereaved, the disappointed, baffled, and beaten, these all require the sympathetic approach on the part of the visitor. Arriving at the door, the visitor should ask in a pleasing tone if it is convenient to come in for a few minutes. He should always respect inconvenient circumstances, and return another time when the way is clear. Entering the home, he should be cheerful, joyful, but never flippant. Other marks of the effective Christian visitor are courtesy, tact, and sympathy. The need and condition of those visited must be studied and related trials and sorrows must be listened to attentively and then dealt with by sympathetic counsel, and appropriate verses of Scripture. Care must be taken not to overstay one's welcome. Before leaving the house, permission should be asked to pray, and in his prayer the visitor will be careful to include all of the family and pressing needs he has heard of. Do you know the story of that "Great-Heart," Philip Brooks, nursing the baby in the tenement house while he sent the poor, tired mother out for a little change and breath of fresh air? We may not be able to do this, but the principle is obvious. Our visitation will quickly reveal how we can relieve the sick or shut-ins, or those who wait upon them.

Prison visitation offers another avenue of service to multitudes of voluntary workers, who usually give some time on a Sunday to visiting local jails. While prisons have their official chaplains and formal church services, the visit of a band of gospel singers and speakers is welcomed by the majority of prisoners. Prison officials are most cooperative when workers abide by prison rules. Whether the prisoners are approached collectively or individually, they should never be dealt with in a condescending manner, as if to suggest a holier-than-thou attitude. While they may deserve their imprisonment, they must be dealt with sympathetically. Dealing with a prisoner, the worker should say to his heart, "But for the grace of God, I might have been in this person's place." As 1 Corinthians 10:12 says, *"Wherefore let him that thinketh he standeth take heed lest he fall."* "Pity is feeling *for* a person," says W. Griffith Thomas, "and sympathy is feeling *with* him." Moody tells the story of taking his little daughter with him when he went out to visit a woman who had lost her own little child by drowning. Moody offered prayer and expressed his sorrow in a sincere way, and yet there did not seem to be much power in it. As he went home, and they were walking along the riverside where the accident had taken place, his little girl said, "Father, suppose it had been me?"

This went like a dagger to Moody's heart, and he turned back and went to the woman with sympathy this time, not with pity, and spoke and prayed with her, and then cried with her in her trouble. When we deal with those who are down in sin, and who are receiving the due reward of their evil deeds, the hymn tells us that we must "weep o'er the erring one" and "plead with him gently."

Workers will be careful never to refer to the prisoners *as such*, or dwell upon where they are. They are only too conscious of what and where they are. Sin and judgment must be dealt with in their broader scope. Above all the worker must stress the love and mercy of God, and the efficacy of the blood of Christ to cleanse from *all* sin. Hymns and solos should be those saturated with the gospel of redeeming grace. Suitable tracts emphasizing the dire results of sin and the way of salvation should be prayerfully distributed. As a testimony is given, a blessed fact to bear in mind is that the last kind Jesus received on the cross was from a thief, dying for his crime, and that this repentant thief was the first trophy of the Savior's finished work.

Hospital visitation also affords opportunities for definite Christian work. The primary aim of any phase of visitation must be spiritual and not merely social. Ministers, of course, can visit hospitals at any time. Lay-workers, however, are usually instructed to restrict their visits to proscribed hours, which they will be careful to observe. Care will also be taken not to impose upon visiting hours assigned to relatives and friends. It is a pity to rob the sick of full fellowship with their own. Further, wise workers find that their ministry of cheer and spiritual help is more effective when they cooperate fully with the doctors and nurses. Both speaking and singing should be of a joyous, uplifting nature. Voices should be subdued. A pleasant tone of voice has a soothing effect upon the pain-stricken. Message or testimonies should be short and to the point. Make Christ prominent not only as the Savior, but as Healer. Dwell upon the sympathy of Jesus and His power to deal with pain and disease. Comforting tracts, or flowers with a Scripture verse attached, leave a fragrant memory of the visit. If, after a short service in the ward, opportunity is given to speak briefly with the patients, going from bed to bed, workers will guard against dwelling upon the physical trouble of the patient, or upon their own hospital experiences, if they have had any. Let the conversation be taken up with Him "whose seamless robe" can be touched by those on "the bed of pain." It is as essential for you to develop a good bedside manner, as it is for the physician. If there are indications that the patient will not recover, then the need of the assurance of salvation and the joy of the Father's Home beyond must be uppermost in the witness of the visitor.

While dealing with this matter of those who are forced to spend time in hospitals, perhaps a word may be in season as to the *solemn responsibility of nurses*, especially Christian nurses, in respect to the spiritual need of the patients. Cognizant of the fact that nurses are primarily employed to care for the physical needs of patients, yet because of their close relationship to the sick, diseased, and dying—a closer and more constant relationship than the surgeon or physician—it is imperative for them to realize how tremendous is their opportunity of bringing the impact of God's love to bear upon the lives of those they tenderly care for. While it may be difficult for them to make time to talk with patients of spiritual things, the opportunity is ever present. It is encouraging to learn of the existence of an Inter-Hospital Nurses' Christian Union, of branches of this Union in hospitals over the land. Such a fellowship is of great assistance to the nurses themselves, and also a source of encouragement to young and inexperienced nurses commencing their nursing career.

Sir Thomas Browne, renowned surgeon of a past generation said, "I cannot go to cure the body of my patient but I forget my profession, and call unto God for his soul." Christian nurses, however, are not urged to forget for one moment their coveted and commendable vocation, but to remember their dual responsibility. Caring for the needs of the body, they should be ready to minister to the needs of the soul. They can soften the blow of the suffering, as with all wisdom and tact and kindness, they exercise a comforting influence by passing on some of the consoling words of Scripture. The following promises should ever be near to the lips of a nurse who desires to do the best for her patients:

> *Yea, though I walk through the valley of the shadow of death, I will fear no evil: for thou art with me; thy rod and thy staff they comfort me.* (Psalm 23:4)

> *God is our refuge and strength, a very present help in trouble.* (Psalm 46:1)

> *He that dwelleth in the secret place of the most High shall abide under the shadow of the Almighty. I will say of the Lord, He is my refuge and my fortress: my God; in him will I trust.* (Psalm 91:1–2)

> *Let not your heart be troubled: ye believe in God, believe also in me.* (John 14:1)

> *Let your conversation be without covetousness; and be content with such things as ye have: for he hath said, I will never leave thee, nor forsake thee.* (Hebrews 13:5)

Often the nurse's face is the last one seen by a dying patient. Theirs may be the last voice heard as the soul passes out into eternity. If, therefore, nurses seek to function as true representatives of "The Lady with the Lamp," as they called Florence Nightingale, mother of the nursing profession, they must then be prepared to undertake a spiritual, as well as a professional responsibility. As patients are so dependent upon nurses, what opportunity they have of laboring as soulwinners.

Nursing is a sacrificial profession, in which hours are long, work is unpleasant and exacting, and the salary somewhat meager. Yet withal it is a most noble calling, and one worthy of the highest respect and recompense. While it may be true that some nurses are merely professional, and that constant association with pain and suffering hardens them to what they see, yet for those who have Christ within their hearts, there will ever be the remembrances that bring His comfort and sympathy to mind, as they share His concern for those who are afflicted, for He makes their afflictions His very own. (See Isaiah 63:9.)

19

EFFECTIVE HOME LIFE

If the activities we have already mentioned represent the circumference of the voluntary worker's life, then the home must be the center of his or her life—and there should be no contradiction between the center and the circumference. However, too often some Christian witnesses are not as *Christian* at home as they are when trying to serve the Lord outside of the home! A motto chosen by two young people, as they set up a Christian home, read:

HERE WILL I SIT BEST!

This is an ambition all should share in their life at home. It cannot glorify the Lord if one tries to be a saint away from home, but a devil within it. Was it not George Eliot who said, "Never follow a reformer over the threshold of his own home." But this should never be true of a Christian! If we name His Name we should be better Christians inside the home than on the outside. Yet, so many seem to be a public success but a private failure. Earnest and loyal in serving Christ during their spare time in the outside world, at home they manifest a lack of Christian consideration. There is the absence of love for those nearest to them. They are selfish, unsympathetic, and thoughtless. They are willing to sacrifice much of their time once their secular tasks are over, for Christian work, yet they forget that it is just as *Christian* to sacrifice a little time for those where they should sit best. Rushing out to a meeting is not honoring God, if one is needed at home to undertake a pressing obligation. There may not be the glamour and fascination about housework that there is in certain phases of public service, but if it is necessary to help an overburdened mother with children, and pots and pans and such humdrum household duties must be done, such service can be made *Christian* and God-glorifying as any avenue of service in church or mission. It is sadly possible to be pleasant to labor within the cause of Christ, yet most unpleasant to live with. How can one's witness be effective if life at home is inconsistent and inconsiderate?

What would you say are some of the essential requirements of a sweet, beautiful, Christlike life in one's home? Well, if those around us are to believe in the reality of the gospel we profess and preach, *we must cultivate a gracious temper.* An uncontrolled temper in a professing Christian creates a false impression of Christ. The sun, however, should never go down upon our wrath: *"Be ye angry, and sin not: let not the sun go down upon your wrath"* (Ephesians 4:26). If, disturbed over something, we give way to anger, we should apologize and seek forgiveness. D. M. Panton reminds us that "prolonged paroxysms of bad temper are a grave peril to any soul: missionaries who used to labor in China declared that such outbursts frequently pave the way for demoniacal possession. What light this casts upon the phrase—*"neither give place to the devil"* (Ephesians 4:27). When curfew tolls, let all fires be put out. A sweet temper is one of the elements of the beautiful life."

Closely related to a controlled temper is a *controlled tongue.* "I will not sing a wicked or a frivolous word for anything on earth," said Madame Antoinette. The Christian with a Christ-governed tongue has a grip of every passion: *"If any man offend not in word, the same is a perfect man, and able also to bridle the whole body"* (James 3:2). Yet must we not confess with shame that too often our speech at home is unloving, harsh, cynical, and unpleasant? Those who love us most are sometimes stabbed by the way we speak to them. Hurtful as well as coarse and corrupt speech can proceed out of the mouth. What we say about Christ outside the home will have greater effect if it is backed up by the manifestations of His Spirit at home.

Another element in an effective home life is that of a *right spirit*, for which David prayed (Psalm 51:10). What is the use of a clean heart, if one does not have a right spirit, which is the Spirit of Christ in everything? Among the things Paul told those spiritually-minded Ephesians they were to deliberately "put away" were *"bitterness, and wrath, and anger, and clamour, and evil speaking"* (Ephesians 4:31). D. M. Panton speaks of this verse not as "a catalogue, but a genealogy, of sin; each of these breeds another and a worse; bitterness—a concealed ill-temper; wrath—ill-temper stirred into passion; anger—passion directed against a particular person; clamor—anger finding vent in scolding; railing—scolding passion into harsh and groundless accusations; and the malignant root of it all—malice, the fixed and settled hatred of Satan himself....If these are harbored, the beautiful life is forever impossible." Surely all laborers in the vineyard will guard themselves against these ugly traits of the flesh and seek to live lovingly and peacefully at home.

Tenderheartedness is another way of experiencing an influential homelife. Is it not as necessary in the home as well as in the church, to be *"kind one to another, tenderhearted, forgiving each other"* (Ephesians 4:32)?

But such a commendable spirit is often conspicuous by its absence. To quote that heartwarming writer, D. M. Panton, again:

> Do we realize the immense stress God lays on Love? Knowledge—the whole range of the Bible; faith—the whole range of the possible; miracle—the whole range of power; almsgiving—the whole range of the practical; martyrdom—the whole range of devotion: it is astounding to learn that each of these, without love, "profiteth me nothing." Henry Drummond

has said that no Christian can read 1 Corinthians, 13, daily and prayerfully, without growing into the likeness of his Lord. Kindness—love in action; tender-heartedness—readiness to listen to an appeal; forgiveness—for, until Christ comes, there will always be, among us disciples, the frictions which require forgiveness:—these are strands woven into the very texture of the beautiful life. And *how* are we to forgive? *"Even as God* also for Christ's sake forgave you." God forgave me, *not* because I deserved it—no more must I: God never rakes up what He once forgives; when He forgives, He forgets—so must I; God forgave me for *Someone else's sake*—so must I. *Our heavenly Father has no friends in all the world today except those He has made so by forgiving.* How godlike! The pure and tender heart is the perpetual fountain of the beautiful life: and our earthly lives, humble and obscure now, will be among the wealthiest things of eternity, if so lived.

A card often seen hanging on the wall of Christian homes reads:

> Christ is the Head of this house,
> The unseen Guest at every meal,
> The silent listener to every conversation.

If such an assertion is true of your home, then all table talk, all relationship between husband and wife, parents and children, brothers and sisters, will be characterized by self-denial, thoughtfulness, tenderness, and love. If the scars of time and toil and pain are the seal of the care of others on our behalf, let us not be forgetful of their denial. Young Christians, zealous in the Lord's work, well-dressed and of good manners, may sometimes deem their parents old-fashioned and plain. Possibly they lost their freshness and beauty in sacrifice for those whom they love.

20

EFFECTIVE MINISTRY TO THE DISABLED

An effective, useful, and fruitful life in the service of the King is not confined to those who are well and strong, and have the full use of their faculties. Certainly the healthy and unimpaired have greater opportunities and freedom in the achievement of great and glorious tasks, but the Bible tells us that the lame are also able to *take the prey*" (Isaiah 33:23). Peter MacKenzie, the English evangelist, used to speak of "the advantage of disadvantages." One of Lord Lyttleton's characters is made to say, "Pain does not conquer me." This is the testimony of many, as Frank Boreham reminds us in one of his essays, "The Handicap." Handicaps were designed not as the justified excuse of the indolent, but as the magnificent inspiration of the brave. The handicapped prove that "*the race is not to the swift*" (Ecclesiastes 9:11).

> *Thy tacklings are loosed; they could not well strengthen their mast, they could not spread the sail: then is the prey of a great spoil divided; the lame take the prey....Then shall the lame man*

leap as a hart, and the tongue of the dumb sing: for in the wilder-
ness shall waters break out, and streams in the desert.

(Isaiah 33:23; 35:6)

While visiting Wichita, Kansas, in Bible teaching work, this writer
was deeply impressed by the nightly presence of a frail-looking woman
who had to be brought to church in a wheelchair. Hers had been a life of
tragedy. As the result of a serious auto accident, she had been left with
a curvature of the spine and will never walk again. A heartless husband,
who was driving the car when the accident occurred but who was mirac-
ulously spared any hurt, divorced his crippled wife. Bright and radiant,
however, this noble sufferer goes merrily on her way, serving the Lord.
But how can one confined to a wheel chair make life effective for Christ
and the gospel? Well, it was from this dear cripple that one learnt of
The Christian League for the Handicapped, with offices in Walworth,
Wisconsin, of which she is a member. It is most thrilling to read the
literature of this wonderful League and to discover the most profitable
ways the blind, paralyzed, incapacitated and bed-ridden can witness for
Christ. These noble souls with afflicted bodies have been learning how
to wring advantage out of disadvantage, and their infirmities have been
made stepping-stones to higher heights.

Many of the handicapped members of this commendable league
serve God in unusual ways. Here is one partially paralyzed for over
seventy-eight years, yet she has earned some forty-seven diplomas from
various Bible courses. Another, once a champion motorcycle rider, also
exercises a wide and varied ministry. Severely crippled as the result of a
spill, and always in much pain, she yet writes a mimeographed letter,
called the "Linnae Blooms," which is mailed monthly to hundreds of
friends. She also raises song birds, and many of these go as gifts to
invalids. Children come to see her birds, and stay to hear her unique
stories of Jesus. Yet another is a permanent shut-in who has learnt to
make her life effective for the Master. As a poetess she has six books
of poems to her credit. Over two millions of her poems in tract form
have gone to the ends of the earth. The daughter of Dr. W. E. Pietsch,
one of the founders of this Christian League, is another remarkable

home-missionary. In July 1944, while a missionary in Kentucky, she was stricken with polio. How she prayed that she might recover and return to her work, but God willed it otherwise! Recovery never came, yet she returned to her sphere in a wheelchair, which has become a mighty pulpit. Before very long, when Jesus comes, in bodies free from tragic handicaps, these noble souls, and thousands like them, will receive the worthy commendation from the Master's lips, "They have done what they could." The pressing question is, are we, who are in the full enjoyment of all our members and faculties, making our lives as effective as those less privileged than ourselves? Read *Ten Handicapped People Who Became Famous*, by Basil Miller, in which he describes those who, like blind John Milton and George Matheson, in spite of these terrible disabilities, achieved fame and still influence the Christian world. Blind Fanny Crosby can also be added to such a list. To those of us who have no impediment the conquest of their physical handicaps is a constant inspiration to give of, and be at, our best for Him who suffered and bled for our sins.

How precious are these lines from the gifted pen of Catherine S. Miller:

OTHER THAN MINE

I would have chosen a sunlit path,
All strewn with roses fair,
With never a cloud to darken my way,
Nor a shade of anxious care.
But He chose a better way for me,
Not sunshine or roses sweet,
But clouds o'erhead, and thorns below,
That cut and hurt my feet.
I have deep joys of another kind,
My Rose of Sharon is He;
And as for sunshine—His lovely face
Is perfect sunshine for me.
I would have chosen my life to be

Active, tireless, and strong;
A constant, ceaseless working for Him,
Amid the needy throng.
But He chose for me a better lot—
A life of frequent pain,
Of strength withheld when 'twas needed most,
And loss instead of gain.
He gave me work of another kind,
Far, far above my thought.
The work of interceding with Him,
For souls that He had bought.
'Tis far, far better to let Him choose
The way that we should take,
If only we leave our life with Him,
He will guide without mistake.
We, in our blindness, would never choose
A pathway dark and rough,
And so we should never find in Him,
"The God Who is enough."
In disappointment, trouble and pain
We turn to the changeless One,
And prove how faithful, loving and wise
Is God's beloved Son.

21

EFFECTIVE SUNSET HOURS

All around us there are those who were once so active in the cause of Christ but who, because of advancing years, feel that they cannot serve the Lord as they used to. Old age is creeping upon them, and facing the sunset years of life, they seek retirement, not only from secular employment, but also from conspicuous Christian work. Able to live comfortably on their savings, pension, or Social Security, they seek to sit back and let younger shoulders bear the responsibility of labor in the Master's vineyard.

We readily grant there are many who can do nothing else but patiently await their happy release from ills the flesh is heir to. The passing years have brought them sickness, disease, loss of sight or of limbs, and while the spirit is ever willing to serve Christ as in the past, the flesh is weak. For all such may an old-time prayer be answered:

> God grant me the serenity,
> To accept the things I cannot change,

> The courage to change the things I can;
> And the wisdom to know the difference.

With age and sorrow and physical ill leaving their mark on face and form, they yet can say with Whittier in *My Namesake*:

> I pray the prayer of Plato old;
> God make me beautiful within.

This homily, for those approaching the allotted span of three-score years and ten, or who have journeyed far beyond such a limit, seeks to encourage those who, although they realize only too well that the years are slipping by, are still physically able to serve the Lord like Caleb, who at eighty-four could say, "I wholly followed the Lord." Do you recall the lines of John Greenleaf Whittier:

> And death has moulded into calm completeness
> The statue of his life.

Life is not to be counted by the calendar, nor measured by the years. We are only too conscious of the fact that we cannot prevent the years from going by, but we can challenge them to conquer our youthful spirit. If the heart remains right with God, enthusiasm and hope will never die. He who is the length of our days will sustain us until traveling days are over.

> You will never grow old if your heart keeps young,
> And your mind is fresh and keen,
> If you look ahead, and can turn your back
> On the things that might have been.
> You will never grow old if your thoughts keep pace
> With the swing of life's swift stride,
> If you keep in step with the stir of things
> In a world that's big and wide.
> You will never grow old if you have a goal,
> And a purpose to achieve,
> You will never grow old if you have the power

> To dream and to believe.
> You will always be young if you take your place
> In the march of new ideas,
> For you'll have the zest and the best of youth—
> The wisdom of the years.

The adage, "too old at forty" is not applicable to those who have served Christ faithfully through the years. For them there are still a few worlds to conquer. What matters, if you are on the other side of forty, is not sitting down and moping! Certainly we love youth because it is youth. We must learn, however, from the experience and exuberance of older men all down the ages that the best is yet to be. Don't be overawed by Shakespeare, who wrote in his sonnet:

> When forty winters shall besiege thy brow,
> And dig deep trenches in thy beauty's field,
> Thy youth's proud livery so gazed on now,
> Will be a totter'd weed of small worth held.

If many winters after forty have besieged your brow, you can grow old beautifully and wear no tattered weeds. Moses, the saint of old, did not commence his forty-year trek through the wilderness as a leader of a mighty host until he was eighty years of age. And when he died, at a hundred and twenty, "his eye was not dim, nor his natural force abated." Joshua, the military hero of Israel, was old and stricken in years when he was told that there remained very much land to possess.

If winter is beginning to settle down upon your hair, accept the challenge of advancing years, and be encouraged by the witness of those who achieved their greatest triumphs well after they passed their fortieth milestone on the journey of life.

If the road of life for you is running through the desert of middle life, pray and labor for the thrill of new beginnings. Live in the prospect of sunset glory. True, the middle years are the hardest and provide a real test for those who are no longer "fat and forty," as some people rudely say. Don't believe, however, that because you are no longer forty, you have had your day and "seen the show." History's most admirable work is associated largely with the names of those past middle life.

> Age is a quality of mind;
> If you have left your dreams behind,
> If hope is cold,
> If you no longer look ahead,
> If your ambition's fires are dead,
> Then you are old.
> But if from life you take the best,
> And if in life you keep the zest,
> If love you hold,
> No matter how the years go by,
> No matter how the birthdays fly,
> You are not old.

Too old after forty? Who says so? Lord Palmerston declared that the greatest things men ever did, they did after the age of fifty years. Sir Winston Churchill, approaching his seventy-seventh birthday, said, "We are happier in many ways when we are old, than when we are young. The young sow wild oats. The old grow sage." Asked which of his works he would select as his masterpiece, famous architect Frank Lloyd Wright, who was then eighty-three, replied, "My next one." All of which proves the dictum of Tennyson, "Youth is confident, manhood wary, and old age confident again."

The French have a saying that the rest of the world accepts and repeats too readily: "If youth *knew*, if age *could*." But age can both know and do. It may be that youth is enthusiastic, ardent, energetic, can study and dare; but don't you be frightened by your gray hair. Maturity has worth, and worlds to conquer for which the young are unfitted.

- Julius Caesar had never been a soldier, never visited a military camp, until he was forty-nine.

- Harriet Martineau wrote in 1844: "At past forty years of age, I begin to relish life and without drawback...I have felt for the first time a keen and unvarying relish of life."

- C. Rossetti published the first collection of his Poems when he was forty-three.

- Beethoven was forty-three when he wrote the Seventh and Eighth Symphonies, and fifty-two when he wrote the magnificent Ninth.

- Blake, the great English admiral, who never went to sea on a fighting ship until past fifty, conquered the Dutch for England.

- Chaucer began to write *Canterbury Tales* between the ages of forty-five and fifty, and died at sixty, leaving them unfinished.

- George Washington was fifty-seven when elected first president of the United States.

- Samuel Johnson was sixty-eight when he began to write his *Lives of the Poets*, and in his seventy-second year when he finished this, his greatest work.

- Disraeli was sixty-three when he succeeded Lord Derby as Prime Minister, and at sixty-nine he entered upon his second premiership.

- Tennyson learnt to paint when he was seventy. He was eighty-three when he composed *Crossing the Bar*.

- Kant, at seventy-four, wrote his great works.

- Cato influenced the world more after he was eighty than before.

- John Wesley preached with power when he was eighty-six years of age.

- Verdi at seventy-four produced his masterpiece, *Othello*; at eighty, *Falstaff*; and at eighty-five, the famous *Ave Maria*, *Stabat Mater*, and *Te Deum*.

- Lamarck, at seventy-eight, completed his great zoological work, *The Natural History of the Invertebrates*.

- Oliver Wendell Holmes, at seventy-nine, wrote *Over the Teacups*.

- Goethe completed *Faust* when he was eighty.

- ✦ Michaelangelo, greatest of artists, created works of genius when past eighty.

- ✦ Voltaire dominated Europe after he had reached eighty.

- ✦ Titian, at ninety-eight, painted his historic picture of the *Battle of Lepanto.*

- ✦ Commodore Vanderbilt, between the ages of seventy and eighty-three, added some hundred millions of dollars to his fortune.

Such an illustrious roll surely proves that life can begin after forty. Approaching half a century of life, men are compelled to consider what they have attained to, and the possibilities that lie beyond them. When he was eighty-five, William E. Gladstone wrote to Lady Dorothy Nevin: "The year hand on the clock of time is marked eighty-five, and has nearly run its course; I have much cause to be thankful, and still more to be *prospective*." Prospective! That's the key word—undreamed horizons ahead. Face them with courage and confidence. Make every passing day and hour count. Make the best possible use of what talent and power you possess, cultivating the friendship of One whose years have no end.

Grandma Moses is an inspiration for all who feel life is over at any definite age. She was seventy-six before she owned her first paintbrush. Now Grandma Moses' designs are collectors' items, and her original scenes hang in major art exhibits.

If you want more inspiration for the years ahead, you can have it. I often think of the story which Sir Ernest Shackleton told in his wonderful book, *South.* "I cannot doubt," he says, "that our party was divinely guided, both over the ice fields and across the storm-swept seas. I know that during that long and racking march of thirty-six hours, over the unnamed mountains and glaciers of South Georgia, it seemed to me, often, that we were not three, but four. I said nothing to my companions on the point, but afterward Worsley said to me, 'Boss, I had a curious feeling on the march that there was another Person with us." What comfort is ours, if, as we know, reaching the end of the march, that the One is ever near who promised, "I will never leave thee, nor forsake thee."

If the years are upon us, may the prayer be ours:

Lord, let me bring a little grace
To every dark and gloomy place;
Let me rejoice that I can give
Some splendor to the life I live,
A little faith when I am tired,
A little joy where I abide,
A touch of friendship now and then
To mark my comradeship with men.
Lord, let me bring a little mirth
To all who share my days on earth;
Let something I have said or done
Remain, when I have travelled on,
To prove the man I tried to be
And make men glad they walked with me;
A flower, a smile, a word of cheer,
Make these my gifts from year to year.

For those still young in years, blithe of step, and with vision and strength unimpaired by age, what better habit could they form than that of constantly recalling the lines:

When I grow old
God grant that every child
Will feel the youthful texture of my soul
And will turn not away from me
As from a shade or shrunken vine
When I grow old.

When I grow old
God grant that I may have some task
Which must be done, or some one fare the worse—
That in some corner of the earth
Some one will need my hand,
When I grow old.

22

EFFECTIVE STEWARDSHIP

We deem it imperative to include the question of "stewardship" in this dissertation of effective living, seeing Paul has emphasized faithfulness in stewardship: *"Moreover it is required in stewards, that a man be found faithful"* (1 Corinthians 4:2). Any phase of stewardship can only be effective as it is faithfully undertaken. This chapter is not meant as a stirring appeal to fill the coffers of any church, but rather as a means of enlightening our conscience concerning all that is involved therein. If only people could be rightly taught concerning stewardship, then the present persistent appeal for money to maintain the work of the Lord would be unnecessary. Somehow there is a widespread misconception regarding the exact nature of stewardship; hence we are guilty of a wrong emphasis in our appeals for money. Sometimes people are urged to give who are not truly saved; and if they are saved, they are sometimes carnal and worldly in life, and with the offering of such, God is not well pleased. The cause of God is holy, and it uses holy things.

First of all, then, faithful stewardship is *biblical*. The term "stewardship" is used in various ways in holy Bible. For example, in Genesis

15:2 we have Eliezer, who was a steward in Abraham's household: *"And Abram said, LORD God, what wilt thou give me, seeing I go childless, and the steward of my house is this Eliezer of Damascus?"* In that far-off day, a steward was a person whose business it was to provide all the members of the family with food and raiment. This steward received all the cash and expended all that was necessary, and of course kept regular accounts.

In Luke 16, you have the parable of the unjust steward, which is used by Christ to underscore the word or term *steward*, for He used that word and its cognates seven times in eight verses. The repetition is remarkable because Jesus never wasted words. He was never guilty of tautology. The unjust steward in the parable was commended not because he acted dishonestly, but because he acted wisely for himself; and the Lord would have us, as stewards, act wisely and diligently in the use of all that we have. In 1 Corinthians 4:1, we have this very suggestive phrase, that those who deliver the Word of Life are "ministers of Christ and stewards of the mysteries of God."

The mysteries here are the doctrines of grace. They form the divine treasure entrusted to preachers, and a treasure that they must guard and also trade with. In Titus 1:7, a bishop, or overseer, as the word really means, must be *"blameless, as the steward of God,"* and there we have a high ideal that the Holy Spirit can help us to realize. In 1 Peter 4:10, we are urged to be *"good stewards of the manifold grace of God,"* and this passage implies that whatever gift or endowment we possess must be looked upon as the Lord's property and used for the promotion of His glory.

Emphasized then, everywhere in the Word of God, we realize that the Lord demands the full, complete surrender of all that we have. *"Honor the LORD with thy substance, and with the firstfruits of all thine increase: So shall thy barns be filled with plenty, and thy presses shall burst out with new wine"* (Proverbs 3:9–10). A similar thought is found in Proverbs 11:24–25, *"There is that scattereth, and yet increaseth; and there is that withholdeth more than is meet, but it tendeth to poverty."* The liberal soul will be made fat.

In Matthew 6:19–20, we are urged by our Lord not to lay up for ourselves treasure upon earth, but to lay up treasure in heaven; and, in Luke 6:38, we read, "*Give, and it shall be given unto you.*" In Matthew 25, we have the parable of talents in which we discover that if we fail to use in a right way what the Lord makes possible, then He will rob us of our stewardship. So, faithful stewardship is *biblical*.

Again, faithful stewardship is *comprehensive*. One cannot study the passages cited without realizing the folly of identifying stewardship with money only. The surrender of our material possessions is a minor phase of the doctrine we are considering. Faithful stewardship covers every realm. It includes what we are as well as what we have and our person before our possessions. Within the range of stewardship you have the surrender not only of money and of material things, but the willingness to realize that God has a definite claim upon our life and service, for stewardship covers every relationship of life. Our goods and our gold are secondary. There must be right employment of our time and of our talents, and then the surrender of our treasures; first our *soul*, then our *service*, and then *silver*.

But, it is possible to surrender our silver to the Lord and withhold from Him our soul and our service. Thus what is needed is not merely the devotion of our possessions on a vast scale but the unreserved surrender of our life that such might be used in His sweet, happy service. It is possible to give our money, and in the surrender of our money attempt to buy off God; and there are those who think that by giving their money they can satisfy their conscience when it is disturbed about a deeper surrender. A person may be a tither, and, yet, not a "liver"—and what is the use of our tithing unless we have a life that is fully dedicated to God? God is the sole owner of all things, and therefore has the right to all. So, beloved, life must be viewed as a perfect whole, and what God demands first of all is the unreserved surrender of our life to Him. This is where Frances Ridley Havergal struck a very deep note in that consecration hymn of hers, commencing as it does:

> Take my life, and let it be
> Consecrated, Lord, to Thee.
> Take my moments and my days,
> Let them flow in ceaseless praise.

The surrender of the life is the basis of all giving. God does not require our silver and our gold and our material possessions if there is not the full surrender of our life to Him. But if He has our life and our moments and our days, then He has our silver and our gold. But no matter what we offer to Him, if we withhold the life, the best we give in material things is useless in influence.

We are not belittling the effective allocation of our money. Right giving is a part of right living. A Christian knows that his giving is wrong if he robs God of His portion, to hoard or to spend it on self. Therefore effective stewardship principles in respect to money are unmistakably clear in Scripture.

1. God is the Creator and Owner of all things.

2. Every man is a steward and must give an account of his stewardship.

3. God's ownership and man's stewardship must be acknowledged by a definite portion of income, giving to be determined by ability.

4. The portion set aside for God should be kept separate and used only in His work.

5. Distribution of separated money is to be prayerfully done.

> To give without prayer is impotent;
> To pray without giving is impudent.

Further, with our Bible before us, we discover that faithful stewardship is *Christlike*. What a blessed and beautiful trait this is in the character of our Lord. He ever practiced what He preached. He did not say to men, "Now you obey these commands of Mine," irrespective of whether He illustrated in His own life the truth that He declared.

If Jesus exhorted men to give, then we can depend upon this that He led the way in giving. He did not say to men, "Give, and it shall be given unto you," without illustration of something of the principle involved in such an exhortation. And this brings us, does it not, to the transcendent truth of His incarnation, when there came the voluntary surrender of His glory—"rich, yet for your sakes He became poor"—and Jesus gave, and gave, and gave, until He became love's bankrupt. He did not have money to give. Jesus was the poorest of all.

We are not told that Jesus tithed, for the probability is that He had nothing to tithe. Although He was the possessor of a vast inheritance, He lived on borrowed things from the time of His birth until His cruel death. Coming among men, He did not have a crib of His own in which to be laid, when He was born. Joseph, His foster father, had to borrow a manger, and as He moved among men, He was forever dining at another man's table. He could not lay claim to any lodging of His own. *The Son of man hath not where to lay his head*" (Matthew 8:20). He rode on the back of a borrowed ass, and when He wanted to emphasize the truth concerning divine sovereignty and desired a penny with which to make clear the truth, He did not have a coin of His own, but had to borrow one from someone standing by. When He came to die, He did not have a grave for burial. He had nothing to leave His dear mother, nothing but holy memories. He handed her over to John that he might care for her and play the part of a son. And so Jesus lived on borrowed things. He had no money to spend, but He had blood to spill, and He spilt it freely.

Now it may be said that you find satisfaction in flinging a few coins upon the plate. You listened to an appeal for money, and God burned in upon your mind a sense of your own obligation concerning the maintenance of some God-honored center; but listen, it is one thing to throw your money on a plate, and to part with your substance in that way, and it is quite a different thing to fling yourself upon the altar with gladness and alacrity that God may take you and use you in His own way for His own glory. Giving your life, you follow in the footsteps of the Master.

We also discover that faithful stewardship is *apostolic*. Read the Acts of the Apostles and some of the Epistles, and you will find them laden with the truth of faithful and effective stewardship. There was a dramatic surrender of possessions on the Day of Pentecost, when those dear men *"had all things common; and sold their possessions and goods, and parted them to all men, as every man had need"* (Acts 2:44–45). The same truth is found again in the fourth chapter, verse 32, *"Neither said any of them that ought of the things which he possessed was his own,"* and they realized as a result of that Pentecostal experience that the lordship of the Lord Jesus involved definite stewardship, that the glorified, risen Lord had divine claim upon their lives and their possessions. We link the two together, for not only did those men have a common pool and make possible the alleviation of the need of many through their surrendered possessions, but with a marvelous abandon, they gave their lives to the Savior, for we read that they were men who hazarded their lives for the sake of the Name. Yes, they followed Jesus in His self-imposed penury.

Think of that remarkable scene in the third chapter of Acts, where Peter is at the Gate Beautiful, and sitting there is a lame man begging for alms. With a look of imploring pity he gazes at Peter, expecting a little money to help him on his way. Listen to the reply of Peter, *"Silver and gold have I none; but such as I have give I thee: In the name of Jesus Christ of Nazareth rise up and walk"* (Acts 3:6). If you do not have a mite to give to the maintenance of the work of the Lord, you have a life that God can use, and that is of greater importance than the surrender of mere material possessions.

When you come to the writings of Paul, you realize that his support was made possible through the faithful stewardship of Christians in Macedonia, in Jerusalem, and in Corinth. Like his Master, Paul was a very poor man. What things had been gain to him, he counted loss for Christ's sake. Thus you find him dependent upon what others could give for his support. In his Epistles you have him yearning for the willing surrender of substance. But this truth is evident as we read the Epistles that come from the mighty pen of Paul, that the inspiration and basis of all giving is not the need of some particular church, or institution, or individual! Let that thought sink into your mind.

The inspiration and the basis of our giving in respect to the church is not the need of the church. The basis for all giving is the resurrection of the Lord Jesus. That is made so clear when you come to the resurrection chapter, 1 Corinthians 15. Read it through, and you will find that Paul is giving utterance to one of the most remarkable sermons ever preached on the resurrection of the Lord Jesus. And you should read right on into the sixteenth chapter, for there should be no break. How does that sixteenth chapter begin? *"Now concerning the collection."* It would seem as if Paul came down from the resurrection to the collection, but no, he brings the collection up to the realm of the resurrection, and shows that the basis of inspiration of all giving is the resurrection of the Lord Jesus. And so he links on the surrender of substance to spiritual reality, and a fuller relationship of our identification with Jesus Christ in His resurrection would result in an outburst of Christian liberality. Faithful stewardship, then, is apostolic.

Further, faithful stewardship is *productive.* "God is no man's debtor." Surrender ever means the enrichment of the life that gives. When we spend our money, we simply change the form of its value. For example, I have in my hand a dollar, or seven shillings, and as I pass a bookshop, I see in the window a book I want, a book I know will profit my mind, and it is marked at the above figure. I go in with my money and ask for that book. I spend my money, but I merely change the form of its value. I have parted with a dollar, or seven shillings; I receive a book of the same value in exchange. But when we give our money we change the control of it. So when we yield our money to God, it becomes His, for immediately when we give anything to Him and to His work, we change the control of our substance. And, let us remember this: that we are called upon to surrender our substance, not that it might become His, but because it is His own already. *"The silver is mine, and the gold is mine, saith the Lord"* (Haggai 2:8), and so we give Him of what we have, not that it might become His, but because it is His by creation, and by redemption, and by every other right.

Faithful stewardship is productive of the highest dividends and of unusual interest. The banks will not give any more than one or one and a half percent. Sometimes you can get good rates for your money. Perhaps one of the best forms of investment is an annuity in connection with the Moody Bible Institute, or a similar reliable institution. But no matter what interest your invested money may make, what is it in comparison with what the Lord will give you for your money? What will He give? *"He shall receive an hundredfold now in this time…and in the world to come eternal life"* (Mark 10:30). So as you can see, faithful stewardship is productive of high dividends. And, not only so, but investment in the cause of Christ represents absolute security. No thieves can ever carry off what you give to God, and no depression can have any affect whatever upon your investments in the things belonging to the kingdom. Faithful stewardship is likewise productive of joy, for giving ever rebounds in blessing. Good givers are always happy souls.

Last of all, faithful stewardship is productive of eternal reward. *"Who then is that faithful and wise steward, whom his lord shall make ruler over his household?"* (Luke 12:42). What do we know about laying up treasures in heaven? God does not want to deprive us of our possessions. He desires us to send them on before. What do we know about laying up treasures in heaven and investing our money in those ways that help perpetuate our influence? Are you investing your possessions in lives, in churches, and in those institutions that make for the furtherance of the cause of the Lord Jesus among men? May God give us grace to convert our cash into character.

The story is told of a good farmer who loved the Lord, and believed in stewardship. He was very generous indeed, and was asked by his friends why he gave so much and yet remained so prosperous. "We cannot understand you," his friends said.

"Why, you seem to give more the rest of us and yet you always seem to have greater prosperity."

"Oh," said the farmer, "that is very easy to explain. You see, I keep shoveling into God's bin, and God keeps shoveling more and more into mine, and *God has the bigger shovel.*"

Will you remember that? God has the bigger shovel. We are so insufficient in the surrender of all that we are and have; we forget that the Lord is no man's debtor. We never give without receiving; surrender ever means enrichment. God has "the bigger shovel," and when we are hilarious in our giving, God is hilarious in His bestowments. So we come back to this wonderful word that Jesus gave utterance to, "*Give, and it shall be given unto you; good measure, pressed down, and shaken together, and running over, shall men give into your bosom*" (Luke 6:38).

23

EFFECTIVE UNCONSCIOUS INFLUENCE

While the burden of this book is taken up with the effective service of those who desire to labor for Christ in their own time, after secular work is finished, there are many who are not called to undertake any public ministry. At times they may bemoan their inability to serve the Lord as others can and do. Yet how effective is the silent, unconscious influence they exert. When Paul and Silas sang that midnight hour in their prison cell, they did not realize that the prisoners heard them, and were blessed thereby. *"And at midnight Paul and Silas prayed, and sang praises unto God: and the prisoners heard them"* (Acts 16:25). Doubtless some of them became Christians, and told the church how, in the dead of night, in circumstances so loathsome, there was the music of heaven. Totally unconscious of their ministry, Paul and Silas sang because Christ was with them, enabling them to forget their bleeding backs and dark dungeon. He was giving them songs in the night, and unaware of the fact, they were inspiring their unseen and unknown companions in suffering to be courageous. The apostles, like Faithful, in the "Valley of the Shadow," lifted up their voices in song because their heart was the home of the Lord whom they dearly loved, and the other prisoners took courage at the music. "He lives unworthily through whom no other person lives."

Yours may be the very humblest life. Your voice is never heard in public. Outside activities for Christ do not seem to be within your province, yet how full your life can become with beneficent, unconscious ministry. Such unconscious human helpfulness can be one of the chief ministries of happiness—happiness which is most effective service. One of the most beautiful poems of Robert Browning is the creation he calls *Pippa Passes*, which is a story of murder and of guilt, portrayed with the passion and the touch of genius. Below is a house of vileness, where vows are treachery and kisses shame. One exquisite summer morning, Pippa passes. She is only an innocent girl, supremely happy, and because she is happy, as she passes, she sings. She has no thought of doing good to anybody. She is quite oblivious of listeners. Yet her simple song of girlish happiness, entering the open casement of the house, comes with the very ministry of heaven, bidding defiled souls to lift their eyes toward the stars. How many there are who, when the shadows deepen and sorrow surrounds them, remain serene and radiant, and who because they smile through their tears, exercise one of life's unconscious influences. It is easier to be tranquil when these happy, resigned souls are near us.

This effective, unconscious influence is often the beautiful and inescapable feature of a sick room. A chamber with a pain-stricken inmate enduring anguish uncomplainingly becomes a bethel. "There is an exquisite service of passivity as surely as a service of activity," says G. H. Morrison. "When the lights are low, when the strong ones bow themselves, when the silver cord is at the point of breaking, you may be serving better than you know."

Further, the world will never know how indebted it is to the real value of genuine and unaffected goodness. "A man may forget all that his mother told him. He will never forget all that his mother *was*." Character can fall upon other lives with benediction. When Sir

Walter Scott was building his much-loved Abbotsford, he put the bowling green in a peculiar place, and at one corner of it built a little summerhouse, where he might sit of an evening after dinner. Why did he erect it there? Was it because the view was beautiful? He told Lockhart, his son-in-law, why he had it put there. It was because he might sit and listen there to the evening worship of his coachman, Old Peter, who was a faithful old Scottish servant, and who would not have talked religion for the world. But every nightfall in the year he took the Book and "waled a portion wi' judicious care." Then he would sing a psalm traveling heavenward to Him who understands Scottish reticence. Sir Walter, reverently listening, was comforted and spiritually helped. Old Peter witnessed better than he knew. It is ever so. Saints exercise unconscious influences in the unlikeliest places. They make a prison vibrate with cheer, and minister to others, unknown to themselves.

For *conscious* ministries we are ever grateful to God, but let us not forget those who know not that their faces shine. Without knowing it, even the shadow of Peter was of blessing to needy hearts.

> If I have faltered more or less
> In my great task of happiness,
> If I have moved among my race
> And shown no glorious face—

But the *if*'s are not in the vocabulary of those who, like Paul and Silas, sing because they must, and who in singing, all unconsciously banish gloom from other hearts. In the word *life*, there is within another word, *if*. But within the life of those who live in the will of God there are no *if*'s. They never complain that theirs is not the conspicuous ministry of others. Unknown, they radiate heaven's sunshine. Frances Fenelon, the renowned French saint, had such communion with God that his very face shone. Lord Peterborough, a skeptic, was obliged to spend the night with him at an inn. In the morning he hurriedly left, saying, "If I stay another night with that man, I shall be a Christian in spite of myself." Fenelon's manners were all unconsciously full of grace, his voice full of love, and his face full of glory. Without realizing it, he was a spiritual magnet drawing others to the Savior he adored.

We think of the noble army of wives and mothers; of simple-hearted men and women whose voices are never heard in public; of sufferers, whose ministry it is to suffer, but all of whom are true to their Lord, who love Him with all their heart; and who, living as unto Him, help heal a broken world. A prison to them is never an irksome cage but a chamber to be filled with heaven's own music.

24

EFFECTIVE COUNSELING

Counselors in campaigns can do effective work in the inquiry room if only they will bear in mind right methods of approach. In an over-all description of personal work, the late Dr. G. Campbell Morgan divided it into three parts—three *D's*: diagnosis, direction, and demonstration.

"It is necessary first of all to find out exactly where the inquirer stands and what is his difficulty. To take a man into a corner, kneel down beside him, open a Bible, point to a passage, and say, 'Can you read that? Do you believe it? Then you are saved,' is the most perilous, almost blasphemous business.

Next comes direction toward a definite *initial* step—that of abandoning the life to Jesus Christ. Whatever his difficulty, an inquirer should be shown that Christ is not merely a great ideal, but a dynamic at the disposal of every man. Therefore, the measure in which the worker is in personal, living fellowship with Christ is the measure in which He will help others to Him.

At the point of demonstration the worker has to stand aside. You are never to tell a man that he is saved. The demonstration, as well as the power, is of the Spirit of God. The last surrender of the soul is to be, not to the preacher, but to Christ, and the first impression of possession upon that soul is to come, not by something I say, but by Christ's own activity, and we must trust Him for that."

First of all, then, the counselor must find out where the inquirer is. In a kind and gracious manner, a few questions can be asked, in order to discover where the seeking soul stands. Questions like the following can be asked:

"Are you willing to be saved?" It is seldom one receives a "No" to such a question. The very fact that the inquirer responded to the evangelist's appeal is an evidence of his willingness to reach a decision. The next question is:

"Are you willing to be saved in God's way, and on His terms?" Attention must be focused upon Christ, not upon self. There is only one way to be saved, as Jesus emphasized when He declared, *"No man cometh unto the Father, but by me"* (John 14:6).

"Are you willing to be saved here and now?" could constitute the third question. When a trembling "Yes" is given, then the worker is ready with open Bible to lead the soul to a definite understanding decision.

The Bible, and the Bible alone, must be supreme in this sacred task, and the counselor should be so familiar with it as to turn immediately to a verse applicable to the need of any particular difficulty of the one being dealt with. Something is lost when a worker has to fumble through the pages of his Bible when dealing with a soul. Familiarity with the Bible is essential.

The prayerful, alert counselor will also stick to the main issue, refusing to be drawn aside in discussion about irrelevant matters. A young man presented D. L. Moody with a long list of questions when spoken to at an inquiry meeting. Mr. Moody said: "I will answer your questions if you will promise me to do one thing."

The young fellow replied, "Right, what is it?"

Mr. Moody shot back at him, "Give your heart to Christ, and then come to me with your questions." The inquirer left the meeting disappointed, but two nights afterward he returned with a radiant face, which told its own story. "Where are your questions?" asked Mr. Moody.

"I have none," the young man replied. "The moment I accepted Jesus Christ they were answered, or appeared so insignificant that they were not worth answering."

It is absolutely necessary for the counselor to have a clear conception of the plan of salvation. Passages like the following are starting points to prove how helpless the sinner is apart from God's plan of salvation (see Isaiah 18; 55:1–3; Matthew 11:28):

> As it is written, there is none righteous, no, not one....Even the righteousness of God which is by faith of Jesus Christ unto all and upon all them that believe: for there is no difference: For all have sinned, and come short of the glory of God.
>
> (Romans 3:10, 22–23)

> But the scripture hath concluded all under sin, that the promise by faith of Jesus Christ might be given to them that believe.
>
> (Galatians 3:22)

> If thou, LORD, shouldest mark iniquities, O Lord, who shall stand? (Psalm 130:3)

When sin is acknowledged, then the inquirer can be directed to texts like:

> The next day John seeth Jesus coming unto him, and saith, Behold the Lamb of God, which taketh away the sin of the world.
>
> (John 1:29)

> That whosoever believeth in him should not perish, but have eternal life. For God so loved the world that he gave his only begotten Son, that whosoever believeth in him should not perish, but have everlasting life. (John 3:15–16)

For when we were yet without strength, in due time Christ died for the ungodly.   (Romans 5:6)

And the Spirit and the bride say, Come. And let him that heareth say, Come. And let him that is athirst come. And whosoever will, let him take the water of life freely.   (Revelation 22:17)

Then they will be made to see that feelings or emotion have nothing to do with deliverance from sin.

One has found it effective to use Isaiah 53:6: *"All we like sheep have gone astray; we have turned every one to his own way; and the LORD hath laid on him the iniquity of us all."* Point out the two *all's*, one at the beginning of the verse and the other at its conclusion. Going in at one *all* and coming out at the last *all*, the sinner can know what it is to be saved.

Urge the convert to go home and tell what the Lord has done for him. As decision cards are widely used in evangelistic efforts, advantage should be taken to secure signatures, seeing they help achieve a definite transaction. The following is an abbreviated form of a decision card Dr. R. A. Torrey used, which the convert is asked to sign and keep in His Bible:

HOW TO BEGIN THE CHRISTIAN LIFE.

1. A frank acknowledgment of my lost condition by nature.

All we like sheep have gone astray; we have turned every one to his own way; and the LORD hath laid on him the iniquity of us all.
                                                        (Isaiah 53:6)

As it is written, There is none righteous, no, not one....For all have sinned, and come short of the glory of God.   (Romans 3:10, 23)

For when we were yet without strength, in due time Christ died for the ungodly....But God commendeth his love toward us, in that, while we were yet sinners, Christ died for us. Much more then, being now justified by his blood, we shall be saved from wrath through him. For if, when we were enemies, we were reconciled to God by the death of his Son, much more, being reconciled, we shall be saved by his life. Wherefore, as by one man sin entered into the world, and death by sin; and so death passed upon all men, for that all have sinned.   (Romans 5:6, 8–10, 12)

2. A firm belief in the gospel of God. What is the gospel?

Moreover, brethren, I declare unto you the gospel which I preached unto you, which also ye have received, and wherein ye stand; By which also ye are saved, if ye keep in memory what I preached unto you, unless ye have believed in vain. For I delivered unto you first of all that which I also received, how that Christ died for our sins according to the scriptures; and that he was buried, and that he rose again the third day according to the scriptures.
                                                (1 Corinthians 15:1–4)

For God so loved the world, that he gave his only begotten Son, that whosoever believeth in him should not perish, but have everlasting life.   (John 3:16)

He is despised and rejected of men; a man of sorrows, and acquainted with grief: and we hid as it were our faces from him; he was despised, and we esteemed him not. Surely he hath borne our griefs, and carried our sorrows: yet we did esteem him stricken, smitten of God, and afflicted. But he was wounded for our transgressions, he was bruised for our iniquities: the chastisement of our peace was upon him; and with his stripes we are healed. All we like sheep have gone astray; we have turned every one to his own way; and the LORD hath laid on him the iniquity of us all.
                                                    (Isaiah 53:3–6)

Who his own self bare our sins in his own body on the tree, that we, being dead to sins, should live unto righteousness: by whose stripes ye were healed.   (1 Peter 2:24)

And saying, The time is fulfilled, and the kingdom of God is at hand: repent ye, and believe the gospel.   (Mark 1:15)

3. A full acceptance of the assurance given in God's Word.

He that heareth my word, and believeth on him that sent me, hath everlasting life, and shall not come into condemnation; but is passed from death unto life.   (John 5:24)

And by him all that believe are justified from all things, from which ye could not be justified by the law of Moses.   (Acts 13:39)

These things have I written unto you that believe on the name of the Son of God; that ye may know that ye have eternal life, and that ye may believe on the name of the Son of God.   (1 John 5:13)

I do, here and now, acknowledge my lost condition as shown to me in the Word of God. I believe the record *"that God hath given to (me) eternal life"* (1 John 5:11). I receive Jesus as my Redeemer: *"Christ hath redeemed us from the curse of the law, being made a curse for us: for it is written, Cursed is every one that hangeth on a tree"* (Galatians 3:13). And as the *One* who alone has power to forgive my sins. *"But that ye may know that the Son of man hath power on earth to forgive sins"* (Mark 2:10). *"Him hath God exalted with his right hand to be a Prince and a Saviour, for to give repentance to Israel, and forgiveness of sins"* (Acts 5:31). Resting upon God's Word, I believe that I am His child: *"But as many as received him, to them gave he power to become the sons of God, even to them that believe on his name"* (John 1:12). I will trust Him to keep me from falling.

At times, common difficulties will be encountered and the personal worker must have biblical answers at his fingertips. Here are a few:

"I am not so bad as other people I know." Show that God's Word is the standard by which he must judge himself, and not the character of others. *"For whosoever shall keep the whole law, and yet offend in one point, he is guilty of all"* (James 2:10).

"*I am too bad.*" The devil has people either too good or too bad. Use 1 Timothy 1:15: "*This is a faithful saying, and worthy of all acceptation, that Christ Jesus came into the world to save sinners; of whom I am chief.*" This shows that God can only save one class—*sinners*: "*For the Son of man is come to seek and to save that which was lost*" (Luke 19:10).

"*I'll not decide tonight. I'll come back tomorrow.*" Emphasize the perils of delay. Show that all God's promises concerning salvation are for today: "*(For he saith, I have heard thee in a time accepted, and in the day of salvation have I succoured thee: behold, now is the accepted time; behold, now is the day of salvation)*" (2 Corinthians 6:2). "He who hesitates is lost." Ask the procrastinator to look at the three "todays" in Hebrews chapter 3:

> *Wherefore (as the Holy Ghost saith, today if ye will hear his voice...)*   (2 Corinthians 6:7)

> *But exhort one another daily, while it is called To day; lest any of you be hardened through the deceitfulness of sin.*   (verse 13)

> *While it is said, Today if ye will hear his voice, harden not your hearts, as in the provocation.*   (verse 15)

"*I am afraid I would go back, or not keep it.*" Show that salvation is not something but Someone, and that we are not called to keep Him, seeing He is the Keeper and must be trusted. "*And I give unto them eternal life; and they shall never perish, neither shall any man pluck them out of my hand. My Father, which gave them me, is greater than all; and no man is able to pluck them out of my Father's hand*" (John 10:28–29). "*Now unto him that is able to keep you from falling, and to present you faultless before the presence of his glory with exceeding joy*" (Jude 24).

"*I have tried before and failed.*" This is a very common difficulty. The inquirer must be shown that it is not trying, but trusting that saves. This can be found in Acts 16:30–31: "*And brought them out, and said, Sirs, what must I do to be saved? And they said, Believe on the Lord Jesus Christ, and thou shalt be saved, and thy house.*"

"There are so many Christians who are inconsistent, that it is hard for me to believe." Occasionally a counselor will meet with this complaint. But inquirers must be reminded that salvation is a matter of personal relationship, and that we are not to be judged by the failure of others. They should be urged to step out for Christ, and by a godly life shame the hypocrite they speak of: *"In all things shewing thyself a pattern of good works: in doctrine shewing uncorruptness, gravity, sincerity"* (Titus 2:7).

"I fear that I have committed the unpardonable sin." Many souls live under such a dread, and are in bondage to their fears. Yet the very fear they manifest is an evidence of non-committal. Stress John 6:37: *"All that the Father giveth me shall come to me; and him that cometh to me I will in no wise cast out."* The writer's booklet on "The Unpardonable Sin" will be found helpful in this connection.

"I am a backslider and am ashamed to return." In this case, the counselor must discover whether the inquirer was really born again of the Holy Spirit. If so, then the following can be used with effect:

> *Turn, O backsliding children, saith the* LORD; *for I am married unto you: and I will take you one of a city, and two of a family, and I will bring you to Zion.*   (Jeremiah 3:14)

> *O Israel, return unto the* LORD *thy God; for thou hast fallen by thine iniquity. Take with you words, and turn to the* LORD: *say unto him, Take away all iniquity, and receive us graciously: so will we render the calves of our lips. Asshur shall not save us; we will not ride upon horses: neither will we say any more to the work of our hands, Ye are our gods: for in thee the fatherless findeth mercy. I will heal their backsliding, I will love them freely: for mine anger is turned away from him.*   (Hosea 14:1–4)

> *If we confess our sins, he is faithful and just to forgive us our sins, and to cleanse us from all unrighteousness.*   (1 John 1:9)

Psalm 51 also reveals the way back to fellowship with God.

Among those dealt with may be what we might call *special cases,* and experience will guide the personal worker in the selection of appropriate passages to meet such need, as a writer on this subject shows:

To those in doubt of future punishment. It cannot be too frequently urged not to discuss with unbelievers the great problems of human destiny until the heart and will are surrendered to Christ. Discussion is useless. Instance such Scriptures as:

> *And I John saw these things, and heard them. And when I had heard and seen, I fell down to worship before the feet of the angel which shewed me these things.*   (Revelation 22:8)

> *The same shall drink of the wine of the wrath of God, which is poured out without mixture into the cup of his indignation; and he shall be tormented with fire and brimstone in the presence of the holy angels, and in the presence of the Lamb: And the smoke of their torment ascendeth up for ever and ever: and they have no rest day nor night, who worship the beast and his image, and whosoever receiveth the mark of his name.*   (Revelation 14:10–11)

> *And in hell he lift up his eyes, being in torments, and seeth Abraham afar off, and Lazarus in his bosom.… And beside all this, between us and you there is a great gulf fixed: so that they which would pass from hence to you cannot; neither can they pass to us, that would come from thence.*   (Luke 16:23, 26)

The Utterly Indifferent. There always has been, and probably will be, a large class utterly indifferent to and careless of spiritual things. There is no greater problem before our churches today than the appalling indifference of the multitudes to the things of God. Here is a call to increased prayerfulness, for *"this kind goeth not out but by prayer and fasting"* (Matthew 17:21).

We should not despair of those who seem to be careless. Oftentimes indifference is only "skin deep" and the cynical smile on the face frequently hides a heart full of distress. The cases cited do not by any means exhaust the objections to meet, but if the work is to be entered upon in dependence on the Holy Spirit, He will so lead and that contact with souls will be for their lasting good.

ABOUT THE AUTHOR

When Dr. Herbert Lockyer (1886–1984) was first deciding on a career, he considered becoming an actor. Tall and well-spoken, he seemed a natural for the theater. But the Lord had something better in mind. Instead of the stage, God called Herbert to the pulpit, where, as a pastor, a Bible teacher, and the author of more than fifty books, he touched the hearts and lives of millions of people.

Dr. Lockyer held pastorates in Scotland and England for twenty-five years. As pastor of Leeds Road Baptist Church in Bradford, England, he became a leader in the Keswick Higher Life Movement, which emphasized the significance of living in the fullness of the Holy Spirit. This led to an invitation to speak at the Moody Bible Institute's fiftieth anniversary in 1936. His warm reception at that event led to his ministry in the United States. He received honorary degrees from both the Northwestern Evangelical Seminary and the International Academy in London.

In 1955, he returned to England, where he lived for many years. He then returned to the United States, where he spent the final years of his life in Colorado Springs, Colorado, with his son, the Rev. Herbert Lockyer Jr., a Presbyterian minister who eventually became his editor.

Welcome to Our House!

We Have a Special Gift for You ...

It is our privilege and pleasure to share in your love of Christian classics by publishing books that enrich your life and encourage your faith.

To show our appreciation, we invite you to sign up to receive a specially selected **Reader Appreciation Gift**, with our compliments. Just go to the Web address at the bottom of this page.

God bless you as you seek a deeper walk with Him!

WE HAVE A GIFT FOR YOU

whpub.me/classicthx

WHITAKER HOUSE